BEGINNING BLUES KEYBOARD

The Complete Blues Keyboard Method

W9-CTZ-612

Beginning · Intermediate · Mastering

Alfred, the leader in educational publishing,
and the National Guitar Workshop,
one of America's finest guitar schools, have joined
forces to bring you the best, most progressive
educational tools possible. We hope you will enjoy
this book and encourage you to look for
other fine products from Alfred and the
National Guitar Workshop.

ISBN-10: 0-88284-938-7 (Book and CD)
ISBN-13: 978-0-88284-938-6 (Book and CD)
ISBN-10: 0-88284-937-9 (Book)
ISBN-13: 978-0-88284-937-9 (Book)

*This book was acquired, edited and produced
by Workshop Arts, Inc., the publishing arm of
the National Guitar Workshop.
Nathaniel Gunod, editor
Joe Bouchard, music typesetter
Cathy Bolduc, design
CD recorded at Bar None Studios, Cheshire, CT
Cover photograph: Karen Miller*

TABLE OF CONTENTS

A compact disc is available for this book. This disc can make learning with this book easier and more enjoyable. This symbol will appear next to every example that is on the CD. Use the CD to help insure that you are capturing the feel of the examples, interpreting the rhythms correctly, and so on. The track numbers below the symbols correspond directly to the example you want to hear. Track 1 will help you tune an electronic keyboard to this CD. Have fun!

00

Track 1

ABOUT THE AUTHOR

PHOTO • C. MARDOK

Tricia Woods grew up practicing the piano in the basement of her family's Tupper Lake, New York home. Her first professional music experiences were as a teenager, playing church organ in the Adirondacks. Tricia earned a degree in biology from Brown University before resuming her musical studies at the University of Washington and Cornish College of the Arts in Seattle, WA. While in the Northwest, she led several original music groups, was featured at Seattle's Bumbershoot Festival and studied at the Banff International Jazz Workshop. Tricia moved to New York City in 1995 and resides in Brooklyn. In addition to leading her group, "Les Fauves," an original seven-piece brass and rhythm section ensemble, she performs on piano, keyboards and sings in a number of styles including blues, jazz and soul. She has played numerous venues in and around the New York area including The Knitting Factory, Manny's Car Wash and Smalls. Tricia teaches keyboards at the National Keyboard Workshop in New Milford, CT.

INTRODUCTION

Welcome to *Beginning Blues Keyboards*. This book is about understanding the blues and putting the blues on the keyboard. It is the first of a three-book series on playing blues keyboards. *Intermediate Blues Keyboards* and *Mastering Blues Keyboards* build upon the concepts introduced here, taking a closer look at specific blues styles and more advanced playing techniques.

To play blues keyboard you must ask yourself, "What is the Blues?" It's a loaded question. It evokes different answers from different people—whether they're playing, listening to or living the blues. In my opinion, anyone can learn to play the blues. Anyone who really wants to play the blues, however, will listen to the music and the stories of the men and women who have played the blues before us, and will investigate the history of this music. It will become clear then that playing the blues is about more than just chords and melodies and rhythms. It will become clear that finding a way to express the *spirit* of the blues through your playing is what it's all about.

Maybe you come to this book already loving and listening to the blues. In that case, it is my hope that these lessons will help you start putting the sounds you already love onto a keyboard. Even if you are a total beginner, you will be playing the blues in a surprisingly short amount of time. If you aren't very familiar with the blues, I hope this book serves as your introduction to an incredibly alluring and inspiring world of music. You might be surprised to know how much the blues is around you already, just because you are here now. Most modern popular music in our culture that was not influenced by the blues. Rock'n'roll came straight out of the blues. Jazz absorbed the blues. Funk and soul music came from the blues. *To play any of these musical styles, you need to play the blues.*

And the best part of playing the blues is that it can be as simple or as involved as you want it to be. You can learn to play a blues progression quite easily. You can also spend a lifetime learning to be a great blues player. On the keyboard, there are a million ways to play the blues. We won't get to all of them in this book. We will, however, cover the basics and take a look at different styles, including Chicago blues and boogie-woogie. We'll talk about playing in a band. When you reach the end of the book, you'll have a lot of the tools and vocabulary you need to speak the language of the blues on the keyboard. Then all you need to do is keep listening, keep playing and keep living the blues.

ACKNOWLEDGMENTS

Many thanks to Nat Gunod and Joe Bouchard at Workshop Arts, to Alfred Publishing and the National Guitar/Keyboard Workshop for making this project possible. Thanks to Murali Coryell, Bill Foster and Russ Meissner for your musicianship, inspiration, guidance and friendship. Thanks also to: Peter Karl at Fifth House Studios; Marshall Chess, Bill Greensmith, John Rockwood, Bill Weilbacker, the National Blues Archive and the Rutgers Institute of Jazz Studies for help in acquiring photos; to Bruce Katz, Brian Mitchell, Dan Cazio and Merrill Clarck for sharing expertise; to Heather, Lois, Caroline, Briggan, Arnold, Andrew and Gregory for bending ears and lending patience and support; to my piano teachers, Joanne Brackeen, Randy Halberstadt, Dave Peck and especially Jerome Gray and Marc Seales who taught me to play the blues first; and to my family for unwittingly bestowing on me the gift of a life in music. This project is dedicated to all of the men and women who have played the blues and have given us this incredible musical heritage.

CHAPTER 1

Music Review

The goal of this book is to get you playing blues piano, even if you don't know anything about it yet. It does assume that you have a little experience at the piano, and it will require you to read music. This chapter reviews some basic music and keyboard concepts to get you started.

THE GRAND STAFF, CLEFS AND LEDGER LINES

Piano music contains notes written in both the *treble clef* and the *bass clef*. Generally, the notes in the treble clef are played with the right hand, and the notes in the bass clef are played with the left hand.

𝄢	Sign for the bass or "F" clef The two dots surround the line for the note F.

𝄞	Sign for the treble or "G" clef The curled part surrounds the line for the note G.

The treble and bass clefs together make up the *grand staff*.

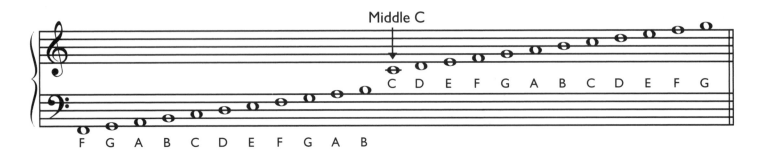

Middle C

C D E F G A B C D E F G

F G A B C D E F G A B

Middle C is in the middle of the grand staff. It sits on a *ledger line* because it lies between the two clefs and is an extension of either one. Ledger lines function exactly like lines in the staff. We can further extend either the treble or the bass clef by as many ledger lines as necessary above or below the staff.

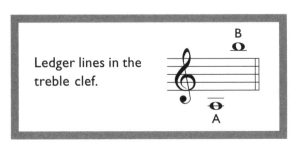

Ledger lines in the treble clef.

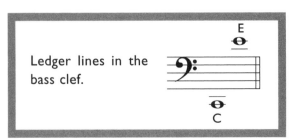

Ledger lines in the bass clef.

THE KEYBOARD

It is important to become very familiar with where notes lie on the keyboard.

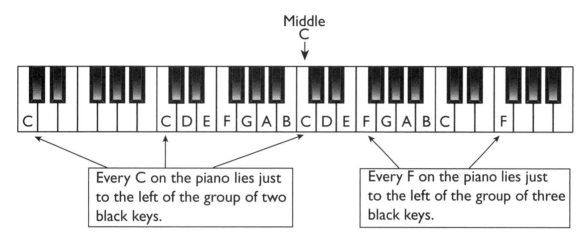

Every C on the piano lies just to the left of the group of two black keys.

Every F on the piano lies just to the left of the group of three black keys.

HALF STEPS AND ACCIDENTALS

An *interval* is the distance between any two pitches. The smallest interval between two pitches is a *half step*. On the piano, any key is a half step away from the key closest to it on either its left or right side.

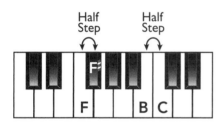

On the piano, a half step may fall between either a white key and a black key, or in some cases, two white keys. There are two places on the keyboard where two white notes are a half step apart: between E and F and between B and C.

Notes written with a sharp sign ♯ or a flat sign ♭ before them are called *accidentals*.

A *sharp sign* ♯ raises the *pitch* (degree of highness or lowness) of a note a half step. Play the key which, on the keyboard, lies directly to the right of the written note.

A *flat sign* ♭ lowers the pitch of a note a half step. Play the key lying directly to the left of the written note.

Accidentals remain in force for the duration on the measure they are in unless cancelled by a natural sign ♮.

The black key to the right of C is C♯. The same key is also D♭!

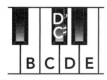

C♯ and D♭ are *enharmonic equivalents*—two notes which indicate the same pitch—but have different names. Which name a note is given depends upon how that note functions in a particular melody or chord. We'll see examples of this when we discuss scales and keys.

RHYTHMIC VALUES OF NOTES, RESTS AND MEASURES

One of the most important elements of the blues is *rhythm* (the organization of music in time using long and short note values). Feeling the beat, or pulse behind the music, and having control over where in time you play a note, will make your playing much more convincing.

Rhythmic notation is used in written music to assign time values to the notes and rests on the page.

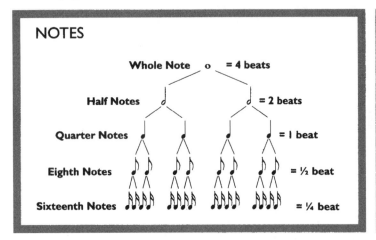

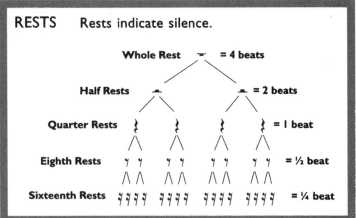

When counting notes or rests that get less than one beat, we need to subdivide the beat.

> Count eighth notes or rests as "one-and, two-and..." etc.
> Count sixteenth notes and rests as "one-e-and-a, two-e-and-a..." etc.

DOTS
A dot following a note or rest increases the duration of the note or rest by one half:

> two beats + one beat = 3 beats ————————————— 𝅗𝅥.
> one beat + half a beat = one and one half beats ————— 𝄽.

TIES
Two notes tied together means hold the note through the duration of the sum of both notes.

> two beats + one beat = three beats ————————————— 𝅗𝅥‿𝅘𝅥

TIME SIGNATURES AND MEASURES

Music is divided into *measures* (also called *bars*) which are indicated in written music with vertical lines on the staff called *bar lines*. Each measure contains a particular number of beats. In the blues, as in most popular music, it is usual for each measure to contain four beats, and sometimes three beats.

The *time signature* appears just after the key signature of a tune and contains two numbers showing how many beats each measure contains, and what kind of note gets one beat.

4—The top number indicates four beats per measure.
4—The bottom number means that the quarter note 𝅘𝅥 gets one beat.

𝄴 is a symbol which means *common time*, which is another way of saying 4⁄4 (the most commonly-encountered time signature).

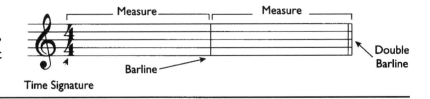

MAJOR SCALES AND KEY SIGNATURES

The major scale is made up of seven notes which, when played in sequence, make the familiar melody: do, re, mi, fa, sol, la, ti, (do). The scale is constructed by starting on any note and following this pattern of whole step and half step intervals:

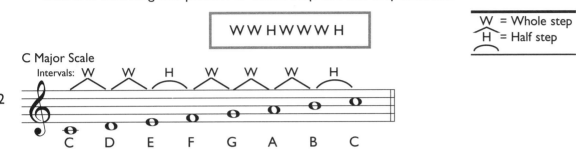

In order to keep the pattern, each scale has its own combination of flats or sharps. On the piano, this means each major scale has a different arrangement of black and white notes.

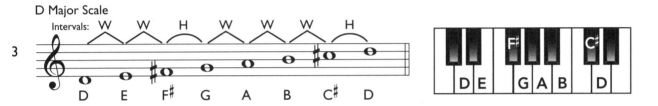

The *key signature* contains the flats or sharps specific to a major scale. The name of the key is the same as the note the scale started from, which we call the *root*.

Here are the key signatures for all the major keys:

The *fingering* (order of the fingers used) for each scale depends on its pattern of white and black notes. There is an easiest way to play each major scale on the piano. Here they are:

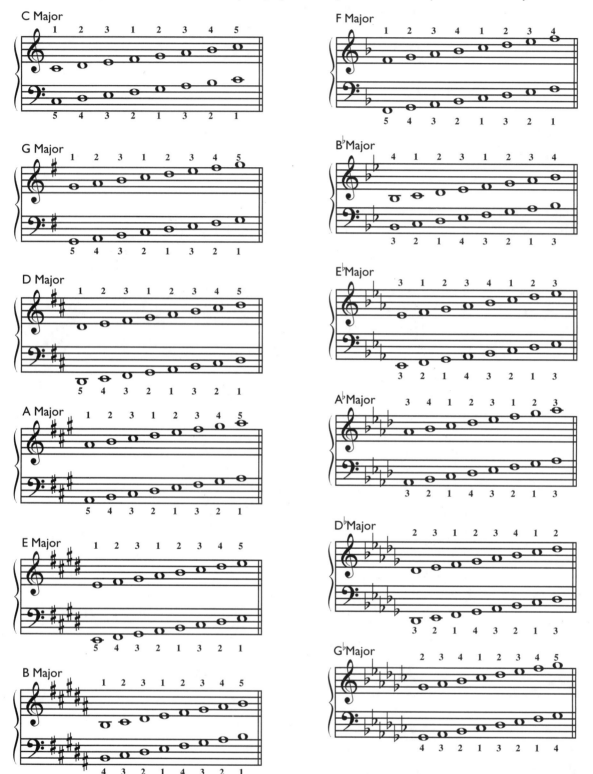

Practice Tip:

A good way to learn and practice your scales is to divide each one into two groups. Each scale will have one group of three fingers and one group of four fingers. Play all the notes of each group as a *cluster* (all together) up and down the keyboard. Your hand will quickly become familiar with the feel of that particular scale.

INTERVALS

All of the different intervals we use in music have numeric names. For instance, another name for a half step is a *minor second*. This may also be called a *flat second* and written as ♭2.

Two half steps together equal one *whole step*, also called a major second, and written as 2.

From C to C♯ is a half-step
From C♯ to D is a half-step
From C to D is a whole step.

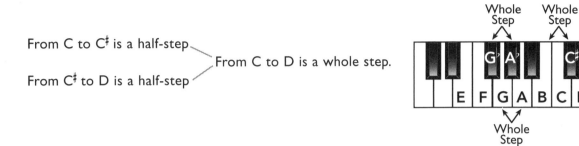

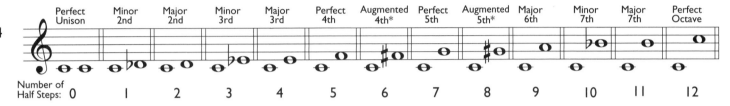

There are twelve half steps in an *octave*. An octave is the closest distance between any two notes with the same name.

THE INTERVALS IN AN OCTAVE

Number	Number of Half Steps	Interval	Abbreviation
1	0	perfect unison	PU
♭2	1	minor 2nd	min2
2	2	major 2nd	Maj2
♭3	3	minor 3rd	min3
3	4	major 3rd	Maj3
4	5	perfect 4th	P4
♯4*	6 ("tritone")	augmented 4th	Aug4
♭5*	6 ("tritone")	diminished 5th	dim5
5	7	perfect 5th	P5
♯5*	8	augmented 5th	Aug5
♭6*	8	minor 6th	min6
6	9	major 6th	Maj6
♭7	10	minor 7th	min7
7	11	major 7th	Maj7
1	12	perfect octave	P8

*If the F♯ in the augmented 4th is respelled as G♭, the interval is called a diminished 5th. If the G♯ in the augmented 5th is respelled as A♭, the interval is called a minor 6th. The augmented 4th and diminished 5th intervals are enharmonically the same and sometimes called a tritone.

INTERVAL INVERSION

Intervals in music are often inverted. The total number of half steps in any interval plus its inversion add up to one octave (twelve half steps).

For example: The inversion of a major 3rd (four half steps) = a minor 6th (eight half steps). 8 + 4 = 12.

> *Exercise:*
> Check your understanding of intervals: starting from a note other than C, see if you can name all the intervals one-by-one and find each interval on the keyboard.

Notice that the major scales on page 10 moved from key to key at an interval of a perfect 5th each time a sharp or flat was added to the key signature. For the sharp keys, we moved up in 5ths. For flat keys, we moved down in 5ths. In addition, each new sharp note added to the key signature was a perfect 5th above the last one, and each new flat note added was a perfect 5th below the last one. This movement is known as the *cycle of 5ths* (sometimes called the *circle* of 5ths). The cycle of 5ths forms the basis for most harmonic movement in popular music.

Since an inverted perfect 5th is a perfect 4th, part of the cycle of 5ths is sometimes called the cycle of 4ths. It's the same thing. Usually, when blues players think "cycle of 5ths," they are thinking counter-clockwise through the cycle—down by 5ths: C, F, B♭, E♭, etc.

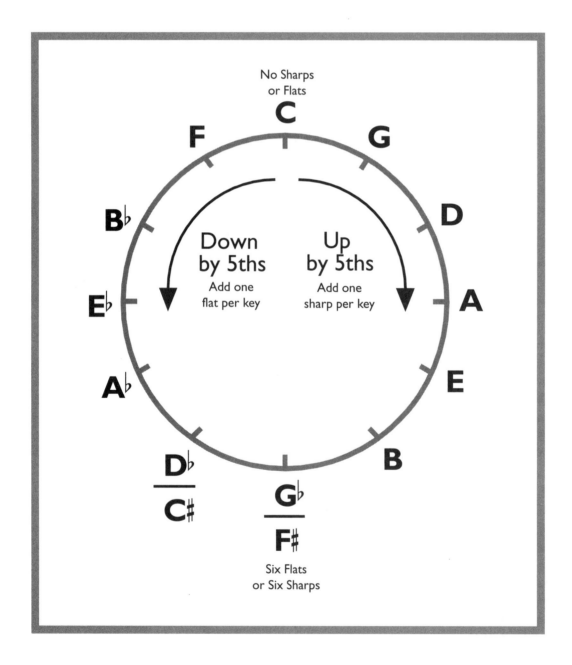

RELATIVE MINOR

Let's look at what happens if we play all the notes found in the C Major scale, starting on the note A. The scale now has a very different sound because it has become a minor scale—A Minor. The key signature for A Minor is the same as the key signature for C Major. There are no sharps or flats in it. For each major key, there is a *relative minor key* which shares the same key signature.

The relative minor key's root is the 6th degree of the major scale.

For example, in the key of C Major, the 6th degree of the scale is A:

So, the relative minor to C Major is A Minor and the scale, called the *natural minor scale,* contains the same notes, but starting in a different place in the order:

The pattern of half steps and whole steps for the natural minor scale is:

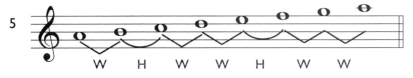

Look at the cycle of 5ths again. The major key cycle is on the inside. The relative minor for each major key is outside the circle. Just like the major keys, the minor keys move up in 5ths as you add sharps, and down in 5ths as you add flats to the key signature.

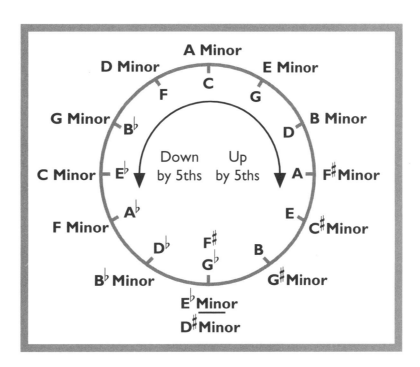

FINGERINGS FOR NATURAL MINOR SCALES

The chart below shows the notes and best fingerings for the twelve natural minor scales.

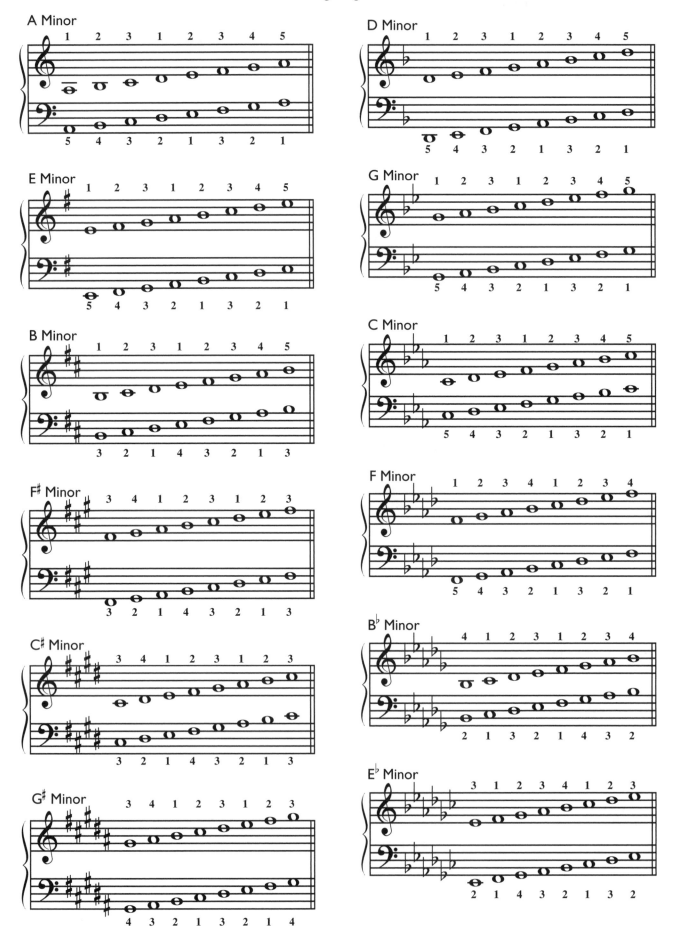

TRIADS

The first *chords* (three or more notes played simultaneously) we'll use to play the blues, are three-note chords called *triads*. Triads are made by putting two 3rd intervals (major 3rds or minor 3rds) on top of each other.

You can build a major triad by taking the root (1), 3rd (3) and 5th (5) of the major scale:

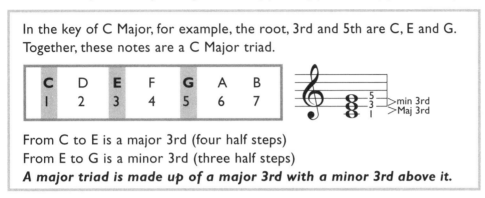

In the key of C Major, for example, the root, 3rd and 5th are C, E and G. Together, these notes are a C Major triad.

From C to E is a major 3rd (four half steps)
From E to G is a minor 3rd (three half steps)
A major triad is made up of a major 3rd with a minor 3rd above it.

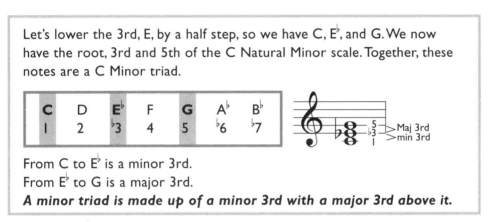

Let's lower the 3rd, E, by a half step, so we have C, E♭, and G. We now have the root, 3rd and 5th of the C Natural Minor scale. Together, these notes are a C Minor triad.

From C to E♭ is a minor 3rd.
From E♭ to G is a major 3rd.
A minor triad is made up of a minor 3rd with a major 3rd above it.

There are two other types of triads which we will encounter less frequently.

Diminished triad — A minor triad with a lowered 5th. For example: C, E♭, G♭. Abbreviation: C° or Cdim.
Augmented triad — A major triad with a raised 5th. For example: C, E, G♯. Abbreviation: CAug

Here is an exercise for learning major and minor triads in twelve keys, going through the cycle of 5ths.

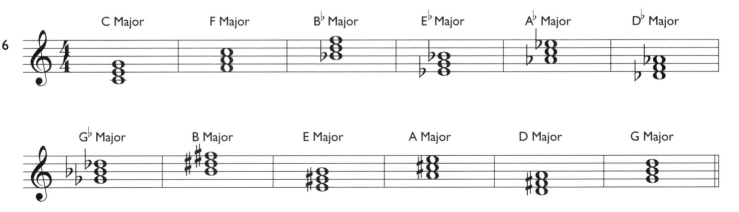

When you are comfortable with the major triads, play through the exercise again, this time lowering the 3rd of each triad by a half step to make it minor.

DIATONIC TRIADS

Diatonic means "of the key." *Diatonic triads* are triads created from notes found within the scale of a particular key.

Every major scale contains the following pattern of major, minor and diminished triads:

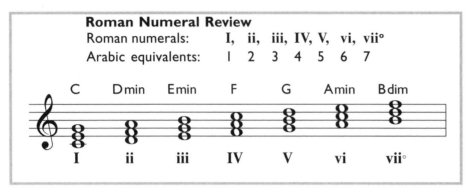

We use Roman numerals to label the diatonic triads according to the degree of the scale they are built on. Large numerals indicate major triads. Small numerals indicate minor triads.

Let's take the key of C and build a triad on each degree of the scale using only notes found in the C Major scale.

C D E F G A B C

From the root the notes are C, E and G—a C Major triad. This is the I chord.

From the second note of the scale, the notes are D, F and A—a D Minor triad. This is the ii chord.

Continuing up the scale we'll get:
E Minor, iii
F Major, IV
G Major, V
A Minor, vi
B Diminished, vii°

The natural minor scale contains the following pattern of diatonic triads:

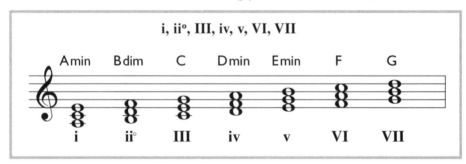

For example, in the key of C Minor (C D E♭ F G A♭ B♭ C), the diatonic triads are:

C Minor	i
D Diminished	ii°
E♭ Major	III
F Minor	iv
G Minor	v
A♭ Major	VI
B♭ Major	VII

Exercise:
Starting with a G Major triad, play all the diatonic triads in the key of G. Notice whether each triad you play is major, minor or diminished. Did you get the correct pattern of triads for a major key?

FORM AND LEAD SHEETS

Measures are the building blocks of songs. The time signature, the number of measures in a song and the harmonic pattern (sequence of chords) through the measures constitutes a song's form.

In popular music, songs are often written as *lead sheets*. In a lead sheet, the melody is written, but the harmony is indicated only by chord symbols over the measures.

Let's look at the following "mini-song" and describe its form:

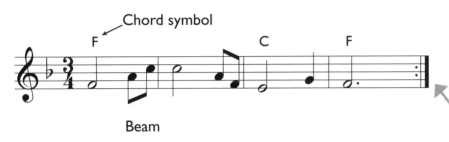

Notice that when eighth notes are written consecutively, they are beamed together.

A double bar with two dots is a *repeat sign*. This sign indicates that the example should be repeated.

The key signature is F Major. The time signature is $\frac{3}{4}$. This means there are three beats per bar, and the quarter note gets one beat. The form is four bars long. The harmonic movement is from the I chord (F) to the V chord (C) and back. The repeat sign indicates that the form is played twice.

Here are some of the various symbols used in lead sheets for the basic triads.

Chord	Possible Symbols	Formula
C Major	C, CMaj, CM, C△	1, 3, 5
C minor	Cmin, Cmi, Cm, C-	1, ♭3, 5
C Augmented	CAug, C+	1, 3, ♯5
C diminished	Cdim, C°	1, ♭3, ♭5

TEMPO INDICATIONS

In this book, the tempo (speed) of the music is indicated with *metronome markings*. A metronome is a device that produces a clicking sound at a specific rate of speed measured in beats per minute. For instance, a tempo of one beat per second, or sixty beats per minute, in a time signature where the quarter note equals one beat, will look like this:

♩ = 60

Now, let's continue and play the blues...

CHAPTER 2

The Twelve-Bar Blues

If you ask someone who loves the blues what the blues means to them, they are unlikely to start talking about chords. But if you're on the bandstand and the leader calls a "blues in G," then he is talking about chords and a specific form. It's the *twelve-bar blues*. There are a number of different blues forms, but twelve bars is by far the most common. Typically, the twelve bars are divided into three four-bar phrases. The second phrase generally repeats the first, and the third is a response to the first two. This pattern echoes the "call and response" tradition of African music which is at the root of all blues music. In a call and response situation, a leader will "call" a phrase and the crowd will repeat it. This became standard practice in African American churches. The three-phrase form was adopted by early blues singers who were often improvising lyrics as they sang. The harmonic structure varied somewhat, but over the years a specific chord progression emerged: four bars of I, two bars of IV, two bars of I, one bar of V, one bar of IV and two bars of I. This chord progression has been in use for nearly a century and is so pervasive in both blues and rock music that it is certain not to disappear anytime soon.

The example below outlines the form of a basic twelve-bar blues. The form is twelve bars long. In other words, the harmonic pattern, or chord progression, repeats itself every twelve bars. Each time through the progression is referred to as a *chorus*. When you begin to improvise on blues "changes," this is the chord progression you will be playing over. In this example, you'll be playing the root of the chord in your left hand, and the major triad in your right hand.

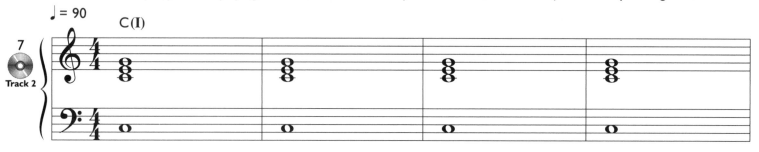

There are only three chords in the twelve-bar blues progression, and they are all diatonic to the key of the blues. They are the *I*, the *IV* and the *V* chords.

TRANSPOSING THE TWELVE-BAR BLUES

Since we know that every major key has the same pattern of diatonic triads, we can use the Roman numerals from the twelve-bar form on page 18 to figure out the blues progression in another key.

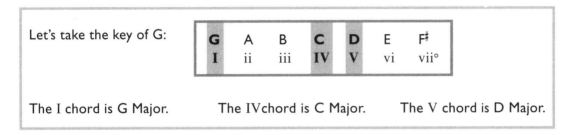

Let's take the key of G:

G	A	B	C	D	E	F#
I	ii	iii	**IV**	**V**	vi	vii°

The I chord is G Major.   The IV chord is C Major.   The V chord is D Major.

Here is the twelve-bar blues in the key of G Major. In your left hand, play the root of the chord on the first beat of each measure. In your right hand, play a major triad on each beat of the measure. Memorize this progression.

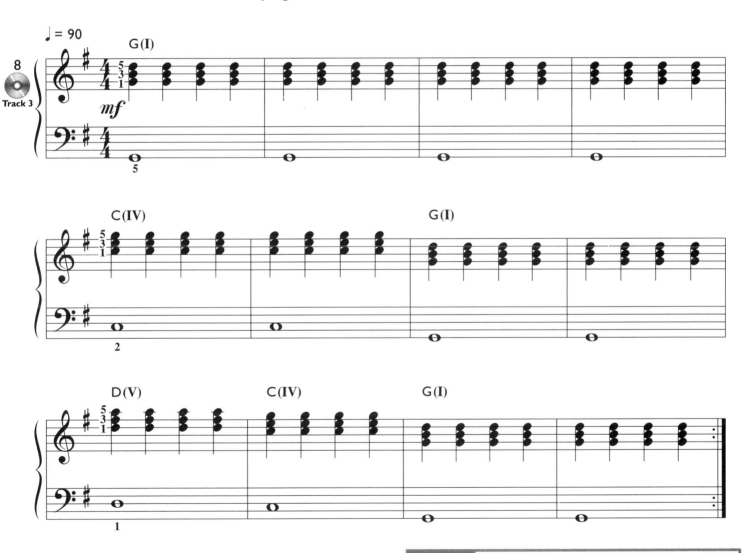

$\boldsymbol{mf}$ = This is a *dynamic marking.* Dynamic markings represent the various levels of volume. This one, *mezzo forte*, means moderately loud.

Exercise:

Transpose the example above into the key of F. Find the I, IV and V chords in that key. Follow the twelve-bar blues form, playing triads in your right hand and the roots of the chords in your left hand.

MAKING A BLUES MELODY WITH ARPEGGIOS

We can make melodies using only the notes of the three triads. The next example is a blues in the key of G Major. Each triad is *arpeggiated*. Arpeggiation is playing the notes of a chord one at a time. Notice the dotted-quarter-note rhythm we are playing in the right hand. Later on, we'll put this in the left hand for some New Orleans-style playing. Look below for help in counting this new rhythm.

Counting Dotted Quarter Note Rhythms

To count a measure of music accurately, start by finding the note with the smallest rhythmic value. In this case it is the eighth note, which gets half of a beat. Since there are two eighth notes in each beat, we will divide each beat in two and count the four beats of the bar as "one-and-two-and-three-and-four-and."

In this rhythm, the first quarter note is dotted, so the second note played falls on the "and" of two. Since the second note is tied through the third beat, the next note we play falls on beat four.

TRIPLETS

Let's make our twelve-bar blues progression sound more like the blues. This example has a $\frac{12}{8}$ feel. The time signature is still $\frac{4}{4}$, but we're going to take each quarter note and divide it into three. In other words, we'll play *eighth-note triplets*. Instead of playing two eighth notes per beat, you are going to play three. Each bar will then contain twelve triplet eighth-notes, which is why it is called $\frac{12}{8}$ feel, or triplet feel.

Let's get used to this feel by staying on the I chord, C Major, and playing eighth-note triplets with your right hand. Set your metronome to about 70 beats per minute and play three triplet eighth-notes on each click.

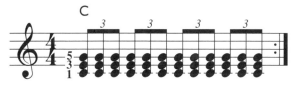

Now play through the blues progression in C Major, playing constant eighth-note triplets in your right hand. Be sure to keep your hand relaxed. Your wrist will get a workout.

> **TIP:**
> All the triads are fingered 1,3,5.

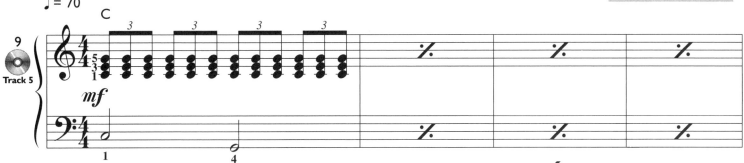

𝄍 = Repeat the previous measure.

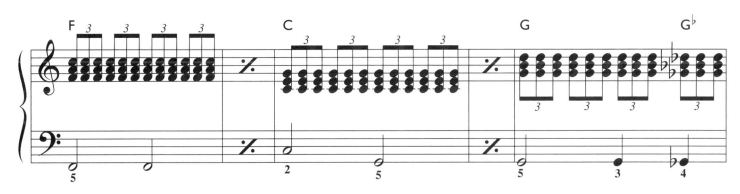

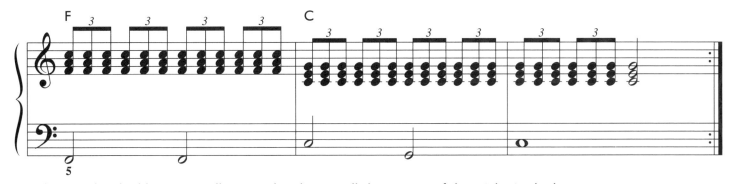

As you play the blues, you will get used to *hearing* all three parts of the triplet in the beat, but you won't always want to *play* on all three parts. Play example 10 again, this time emphasizing the first and third eighth note of each beat, and "ghosting" the second note so that you barely hear it. It's worth your time to get comfortable with this feel. It's an integral part of blues keyboard playing.

INVERTING TRIADS

So far we've been playing all of our triads in root position. In other words, the root of the chord is the lowest note in the chord, the 3rd is next and the 5th is the highest. We have more sounds to choose from if we rearrange the position of the notes in the chords. This is called *inverting* the triads.

Every triad has three positions:

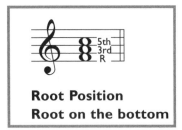

Root Position
Root on the bottom

1st Inversion
3rd on the bottom

2nd Inversion
5th on the bottom

R = Root

> Inversions are used to create good *voice leading* in a chord progression   The goal of good voice leading is to create smooth melodic movements in the different voices. Each note of a chord can be thought of as a voice in a choir. As we move from chord to chord, each voice moves to its next note. For instance, all the top notes in the chords comprise the highest voice. As the harmonies you play get more complex, it will become more and more important to pay attention to voice leading.

Let's look at a twelve-bar blues in F Major to see how we might use inversions.

The I chord sounds strong with the root as its top note, so we'll start with F Major in first inversion. We can then play the B♭ chord (IV) in root position without having to move our hand very much. This creates a smoother sound at the chord change, especially since the top note of the chord doesn't change. For the C chord, we'll play another root position triad because it's just a whole step away, and then back to the F chord in 1st inversion.

In this example, play the triads with your right hand and with your left hand, play the root of the chord on beat one of each measure.

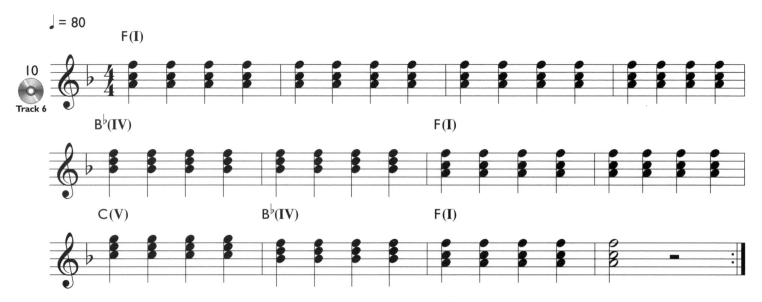

Notice that the left hand part is not written out in the music. This is common in blues, jazz and pop music. If you use any music at all, it is likely to be a *lead sheet*, with melody and chord names only. The rest is up to you. In this case it's easy. You know from the name of the chord, which is the name of the root note. Play root whole notes in the left hand.

INVERSION EXCERCISES

If you're going to play the blues in different keys and use inversions that sound good, you need to have all of the triads right under your fingers. Let's look at some exercises to learn triads.

1. Play root position triads down through the cycle of 5ths, holding each chord for four beats. Start on C, then play G, then D, etc. See page 12 to review the cycle of 5ths.

2. Play the two exercises below.

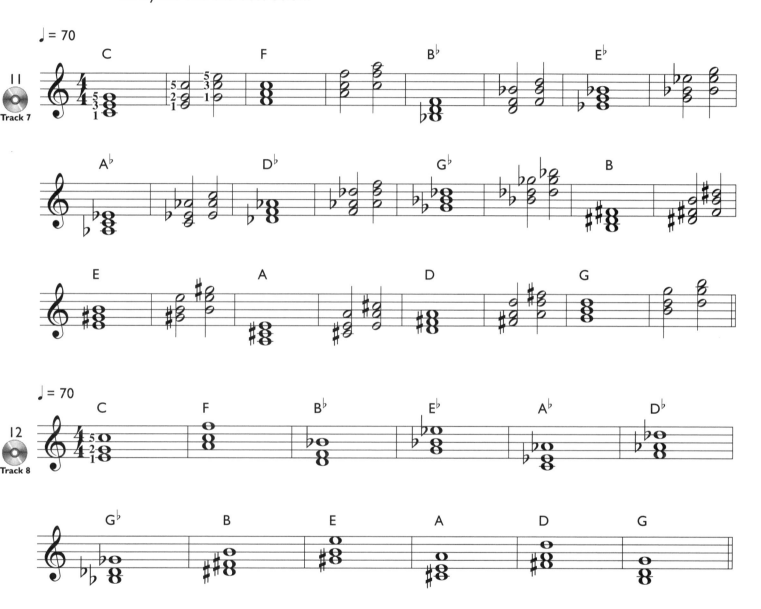

3. Following the format of example 13, play 2nd inversion triads through the cycle of 5ths, holding each chord for four beats.

Practice Tip:
• Play with a metronome. That way you are working on your rhythm all the time. • Practice slowly. Give your ears and hand and brain time to absorb new information. • Practice without looking at the page. These exercises are designed only to get you started. The blues is not a "reading" kind of music. It is most important to hear what you are doing.

It's time to get the left hand working harder. This is a typical *shuffle* bass pattern using triplets in the right hand. It also uses the triplet feel in the left hand, but instead of being notated as triplets it's shown as eighth notes with an indication that the eighths are *swung*. The marking, *Swing 8ths* means that the first eighth note of each beat is held longer than the second. Imagine accenting the first and third of three triple eighth notes like you did on page 21.

Play through the next song with just your left hand.

Now you are ready to add the right-hand part. The right hand is playing three triple eighth notes triplets per beat. So, the second eighth note in the left hand coincides with the third eighth note in the right-hand triplet. If this seems tricky at first, don't worry. You will have lots of opportunity to practice it throughout this book, and it will become easy.

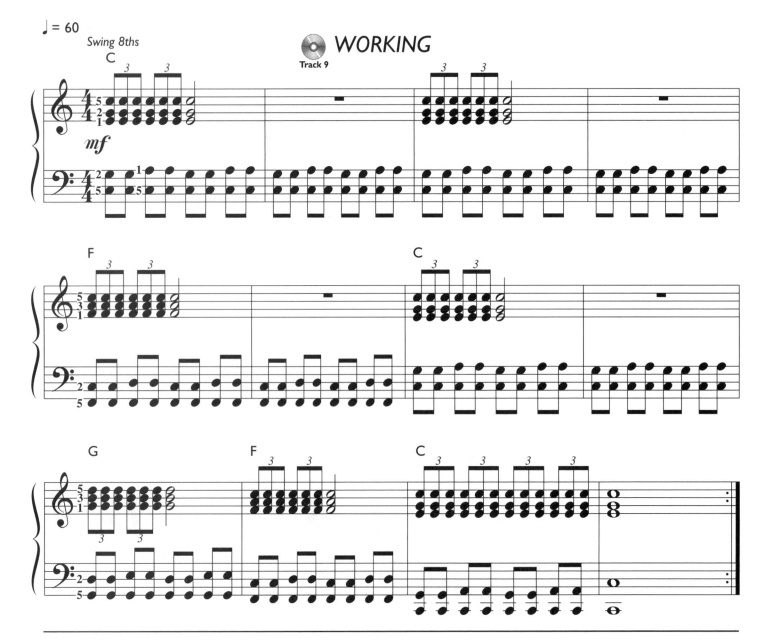

Roosevelt "The Honeydripper" Sykes,
*born in 1906, was equally gifted as a blues pianist,
songwriter and singer. He frequently sang while he
played, but also accompanied many great blues
vocalists. Roosevelt began his career in St. Louis at the
age of 14, ran away to play in barrelhouses in
Mississippi and Louisiana when he was 15, and made
his first recording for Okeh records in New York at the
age of 23. He later spent a great deal of time in
Chicago where he was an integral part of the Chicago
blues scene, influencing many young pianists, especially
Memphis Slim. Listen to blues by Roosevelt "The
Honeydripper" Sykes on Smithsonian/Folkways
recordings for some incredible playing, including
examples of the shuffle bass pattern you just learned.*

Practice this pattern through the descending cycle of 5ths.
Here is an exercise to take you through six keys:

Now play the other six keys to finish the cycle of 5ths: G♭, B, E, A, D and G.

Sometimes the twelve-bar blues is played in a minor key. Look at what happens when we take diatonic triads from the natural minor to make a twelve-bar blues.

Let's start with the key of A Minor:

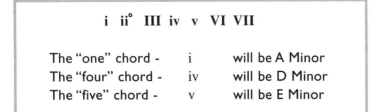

A	B	C	D	E	F	G
1	2	3	4	5	6	7

The pattern of diatonic triads for minor keys is:

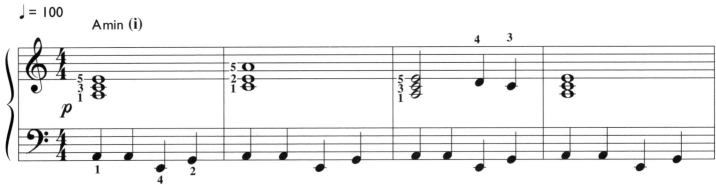

i ii° III iv v VI VII

The "one" chord -   i   will be A Minor
The "four" chord -   iv   will be D Minor
The "five" chord -   v   will be E Minor

Here is a minor blues using inversions of minor triads. Play the bass line alone first.

p = Piano. Soft.

MELANCHOLY BLUE

Track 11

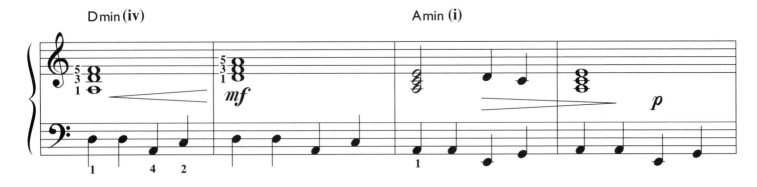

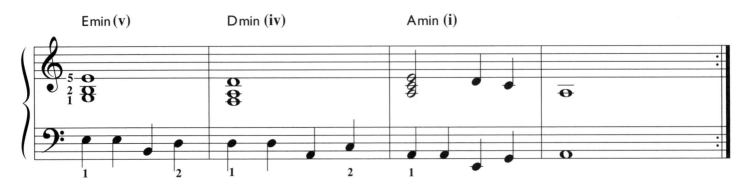

FUNKY THUNKY

This minor blues has an eighth-note pattern in the left hand which is played in straight eighths rather than swung. This means that all the eighth notes are of equal time value. The resulting feel is more like funk or rock.

Remember, the key of C Minor has three flat notes: B♭, E♭ and A♭.

Notice how almost all of the melody notes in this blues outline the minor triads. In the next chapter we will look at blues melodies in more detail. Your left hand is introduced to a new bass line. It is comprised entirely of roots, but in alternating octaves. This type of bass line is very common.

FUNKY THUNKY

Track 12

𝆑 = Forte. Loud.

Exercise:

Transpose this blues into the key of A Minor. Start by writing out the chord progression (use Roman numerals). Your left hand will play the roots of the chords. Your right hand will mainly outline inversions of the triads. You're on your way to playing the blues in twelve keys!

MAJOR CHORDS IN THE MINOR BLUES

A minor blues always starts on a minor chord, but quite often the V chord is major instead of minor, and sometimes both the IV and the V chords are major. This is the case in the next blues, which uses the same shuffle bass line we learned on page 24. The feel for this blues is swing eighths. Both the melody and the bass line are swung.

Look out—this blues is in B Minor, one of the saddest keys.

WORRYING BLUES

Track 13

Without thinking about it, you probably noticed that a minor blues has a darker, or sadder sound than a major blues. Different musical sounds evoke different emotional responses in us. It's important to learn to trust your instincts about sound so you will choose what you play to convey a feeling, rather than to follow a rule.

WRITE YOUR OWN TWELVE-BAR BLUES

It's time to be the composer and write your own blues tune.

Below is a list of all the concepts we've been talking about. Choose any of them for your blues composition.

Major triads

Minor triads

Triads in first or second inversion

Straight eighth-note feel vs. swing eighths

Playing constant eighth-note triplets

Making triads into a melody (arpeggiation)

Bass lines:
    Playing the root
    Playing the root in octaves
    Shuffle style bass line

A few questions to get you started:

Will it be major or minor?
    (If minor, will the IV and V chords be minor or major?)
What key will it be in?
Which feel will the bass line have? Swing or Straight Eighths?
Will the right hand play chords, a single-note melody or both?
What will be the inversion of the first chord?
Have fun!

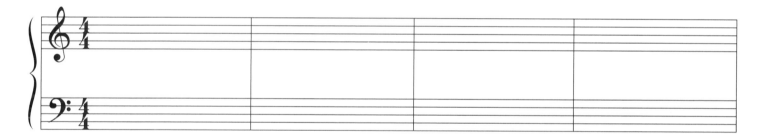

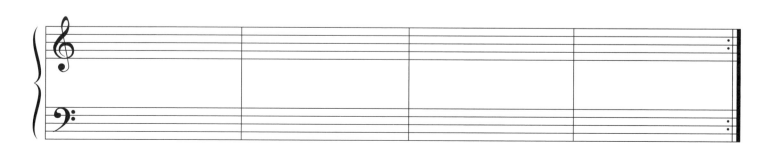

CHAPTER 3

Blues Melodies

"The blues are almost sacred to some
people, but others don't understand..."
B.B. King

Let's investigate how blues melodies are made. First of all, we have to remember that the blues developed as vocal music. The whole point of playing the blues is having a story or feeling to communicate. If we think about singing a song as we create a blues melody, we cannot go too far wrong.

Secondly, you have learned that the blues form has a specific sound. The combination of blues harmonies with certain melody notes creates sounds which clearly say "I've got the blues." In this chapter, you will become familiar with these sounds so that, in making blues melodies, you can capture the feeling that best tells your story.

We saw earlier that, by arpeggiating triads, it's possible to compose a blues melody solely from chord tones. This is fine, and as a starting point it's good to notice that *chord tones work as melody notes.* However, our goal is to get to the heart of the blues, and we wouldn't get very far with only the root, 3rd and 5th.

When people with backgrounds in European music first heard the blues being sung, they didn't know how to describe it because they heard pitches that didn't fit scales as they knew them. Over time, African influences blended with European influences and these pitches, called *blue notes,* came to be uniformly described as notes lowered from the major scale by a half step. Blues singers still sang pitches "between" the notes, and blues guitarists would frequently "bend" notes. On an instrument like the piano, however, or on paper, the best one could do was approximate these sounds by adding blue notes to scales they already knew. There are commonly three blue notes: the lowered 3rd ($\flat$3), the lowered 5th ($\flat$5), and the lowered 7th ($\flat$7).

In the key of C the notes are:	C	D	E	F	G	A	B
The blue notes are:			E$\flat$		G$\flat$		B$\flat$

We end up with a whole lot of notes to choose from for our blues melodies. Let's look at the key of C:

Notes for Blues Melodies in C								
C	D	(E$\flat$)	E	F	(G$\flat$)	G	A	(B$\flat$)	C
1	2	($\flat$3)	3	4	($\flat$5)	5	6	($\flat$7)	1

Some people call all of these notes together the *blues scale.* However, the term "blues scale" is more often used to refer to a subset of these notes. There are a few simpler scales contained within this group of notes and you will become familiar with them in this chapter.

TRANSPOSING THE TWELVE-BAR BLUES

Bessie Smith, "Empress of the Blues," was an extraordinary talent. A strong, hypnotic performer, Bessie was so good at conjuring her audience that her style was compared to Southern preachers. At the same time, she was capable of working with the finest jazz musicians, and is credited with moving the blues from a rural-countrified art form to a more sophisticated and urban blues-jazz blend. She rose from a childhood of extreme poverty and hardship to become the most popular black entertainer of her time.

Drowning in My Blues is in the style of *Backwater Blues*, a classic Bessie Smith tune which has been covered by several other performers.

DROWNING IN MY BLUES

So much sor-row on my mind,——— Lord, I don't know what— to— do.

So much sor-row on my mind,——— Lord, I don't know what— to— do.

'Cause it's rain-ing— all the time—— I think I'm drown-ing in my blues.

* Go back to the first repeat sign and play again.

Notice the characteristic structure and content that make this a classic blues example.

- Three lyrical phrases. The first one is repeated. The third is a *response* to the first two.

- Three corresponding melodic phrases, set apart from each other by *space*.

- Each melodic phrase has a clear shape.

- Each melodic phrase contains chord tones and blue notes.

THE MAJOR PENTATONIC SCALE

Within the set of notes for blues melodies shown on page 30 are some more simplified scales, each of which gives a particular flavor to the blues. Two of these scales are the major and minor pentatonic scales. These scales get the name "pentatonic" from the fact that they are five-note scales. ("Penta" is the Greek word for "five." The major and natural minor scales are seven note scales.)

Here is the "formula" for the major pentatonic scale, along with the corresponding notes in the key of C:

1	2	3	5	6
C	D	E	G	A

The scale has a major sound because the 3rd, E, is a major 3rd (four half steps above the root—see the interval chart on page 11).

The best way to practice pentatonic scales on the keyboard is to play them over three octaves with fingerings that span two octaves.

TWO-OCTAVE FINGERINGS FOR MAJOR PENTATONIC SCALES

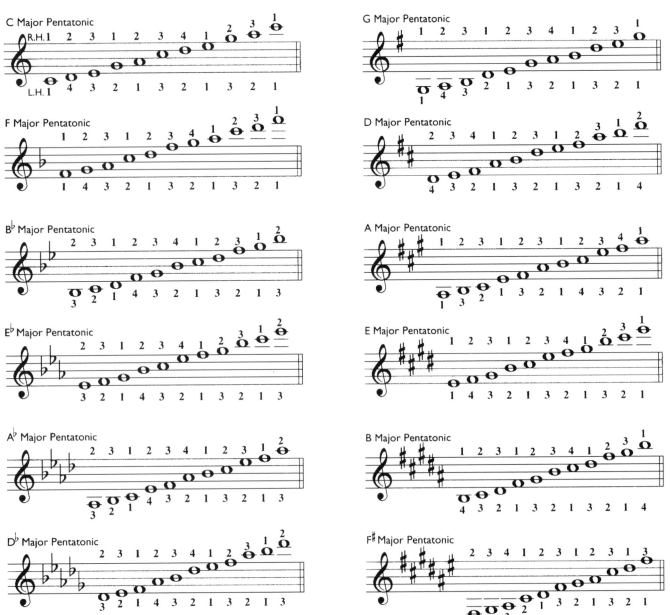

Here's a major blues for you to learn.

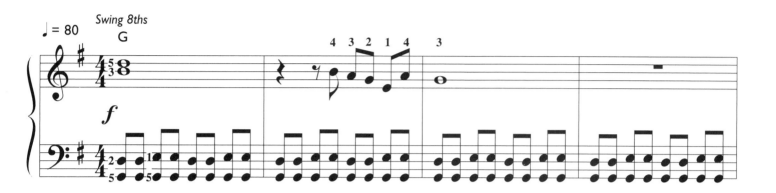

THE MAJOR'S BLUES

Track 14

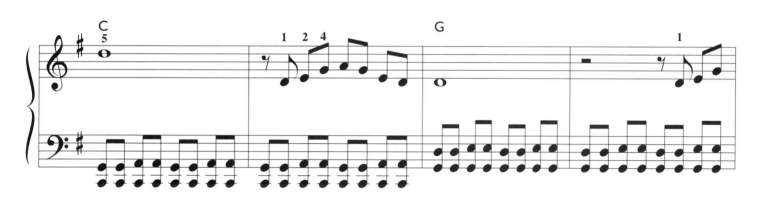

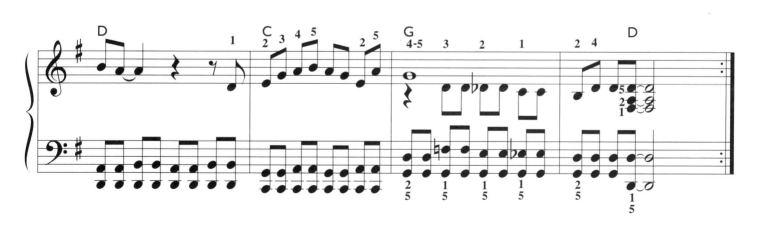

Just as for every major scale there is a relative minor scale (see page 13), for every major pentatonic scale there is a relative minor pentatonic scale. The root of the relative minor key is a 6th above the root of the major key.

Major Pentatonic Formula:	1	2	3	5	6	1
C Major Pentatonic:	C	D	E	G	A	C
A Minor Pentatonic:			A	C	D	E	G	(A)

Numbering the notes of the minor pentatonic relative to its root gives us a new formula:

A	C	D	E	G
1	♭3	4	5	♭7

Let's find the notes of the C Minor Pentatonic:

C	E♭	F	G	B♭
1	♭3	4	5	♭7

The C Minor Pentatonic scale contains two blue notes for the key of C: E♭ and B♭. It also contains chord tones from all three triads used in a C blues progression. Listen to how a C blues sounds when the melody is taken from the C Minor Pentatonic scale.

🎵 THE MINER'S BLUES
Track 15

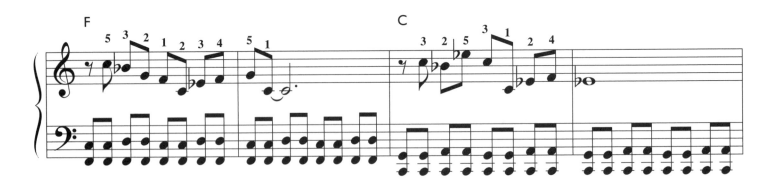

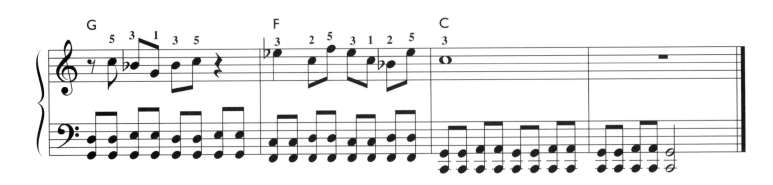

Review the pentatonic scale formula:

> **Minor Pentatonic Scale Formula**
> 1 ♭3 4 5 ♭7

> **Major Pentatonic Scale Formula**
> 1 2 3 5 6

Stevie Ray Vaughan came to prominence in the 1970s and '80s. He took soloing with pentatonic scales to new heights. Listen to his strongly minor pentatonic flavored playing on "Texas Flood" (Epic Records).

TWO-OCTAVE FINGERINGS FOR THE MINOR PENTATONIC SCALES

A Minor Pentatonic

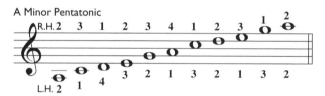

E Minor Pentatonic

D Minor Pentatonic

B Minor Pentatonic

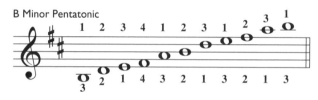

G Minor Pentatonic

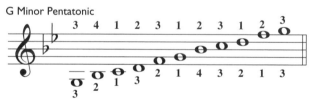

F# Minor Pentatonic

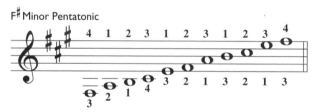

C Minor Pentatonic

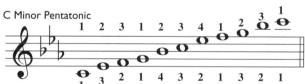

C# Minor Pentatonic

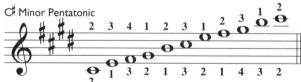

F Minor Pentatonic

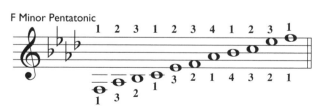

G# Minor Pentatonic

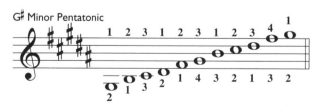

B♭ Minor Pentatonic

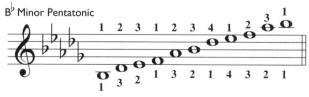

D# Minor Pentatonic

DOMINANT 7TH CHORDS

So far, the chords we've used to play the blues have been triads—three-note chords containing the root, 3rd and 5th of the scale they are from.

Now we're going to add one more note to the chords to make them 7th chords. Let's look at the notes of the major scale again, and this time, notice every other note:

C	D	E	F	G	A	B
1	2	3	4	5	6	7

We can use every other note of the scale to build a four-note chord:

To make a C Dominant 7th chord, or **C7**, we lower the major 7th by a half step from B to B♭ (♭7).

C	E	G	B
1	3	5	7

This is a **C Major 7** chord.

C	E	G	B♭
1	3	5	♭7

This is a **C7** chord.

Practice playing dominant 7th chords in root position around the cycle of 5ths. Play the root of each chord in your left hand.

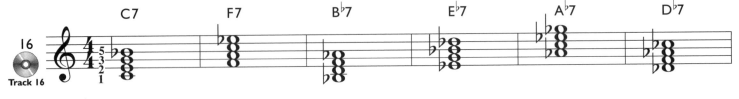

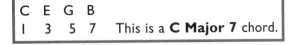

This exercise gets you playing dominant chords in your left hand. Before you start, play a C7 chord with your left hand starting on C one octave below middle C on the piano. Now play C, E and B♭, but leave out the G. It sounds almost exactly the same, but less "muddy," or cluttered. Piano players have to be careful of playing too many notes, too close together in the lower ranges of the piano. Sometimes you can leave a note out of a chord, and still get the same sound. In this exercise you will leave out the 5th, playing only the 1, 3 and ♭7 of each chord.

Another way to understand dominant 7th chords is to build them from the major scale in which their root is the 5th degree. For example, C is the 5th degree of F Major. So build a C7 chord by taking every other note of the F Major scale starting on C.

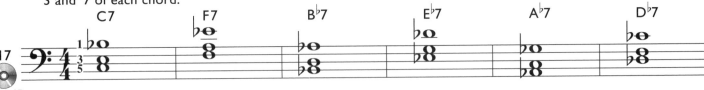

Position in scale:	1	2	3	4	5	6	7	1	2	3	4...
F Major scale:	F	G	A	B♭	C	D	E	F	G	A	B♭...
C7 chord:					C		E		G		B♭
Position in chord:					1		3		5		♭7

THE BLUES SCALE

We can make the minor pentatonic scale bluesier by adding one more note to it—the keyboard player's favorite blue note—the ♭5. This scale is often called *the blues scale*.

Here is the C Blues scale:

The Formula:	I	♭3	4	♭5	5	♭7
In C:	C	E♭	F	G♭	G	B♭

Since it includes all three blue notes, the ♭3, ♭5 and ♭7, this scale is going to provide you with a lot of great blues sounds. Some of your favorite licks will come out of this scale, so you should learn it very well in all twelve keys.

RIGHT-HAND FINGERINGS FOR THE BLUES SCALE IN TWELVE KEYS

Since the blues scale contains six notes, each one-octave fingering has either two groups of three (1-2-3, 1-2-3) or a group of two and a group of four (1-2, 1-2-3-4). You can practice blues scales just like you practiced major scales (see the Practice Tip on the bottom of page 10).

Blues Scale Formula:
I ♭3 4 ♭5 5 ♭7

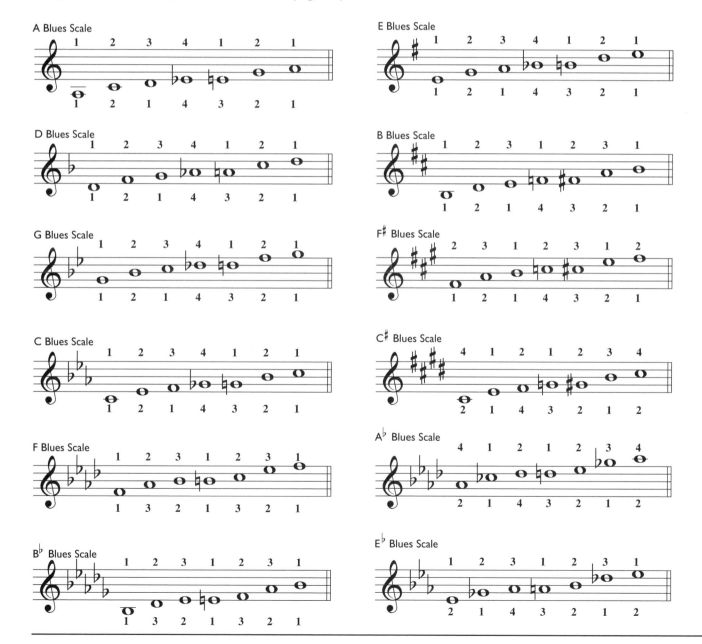

Dominant 7th chords create tension in a chord progression. Let's see why:

Within the notes of every dominant 7th chord is an interval called a *tritone*, which is another name for a diminished 5th or augmented 4th (a distance of six half steps).

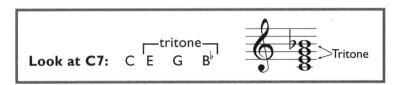

Look at C7: C E G B♭

The interval from E to B♭ is a tritone. Played together, E and B♭ create a very *unresolved* or *tense* sound. Your ear wants to hear one or both of the notes move somewhere. Play E and B♭ together, then move each note in by one half-step to F and A.

You have just resolved the very unstable sound of a tritone to a stable sounding major 3rd. This type of resolution is the basis of most harmonic movement in our culture. Blues harmony is unique in that it frequently is based solely on dominant chords. The harmonic movement is from one dominant 7th chord to another and the tritone never fully resolves.

In this blues, you'll play dominant 7th chords in your left hand, and melodies from the blues scale in your right hand. In addition to the tension within each dominant 7th chord, you'll find some interesting dissonances (clashes) between the chord tones in your left hand and some of the right-hand melody notes. Welcome to the blues!

GET TO IT

Track 18

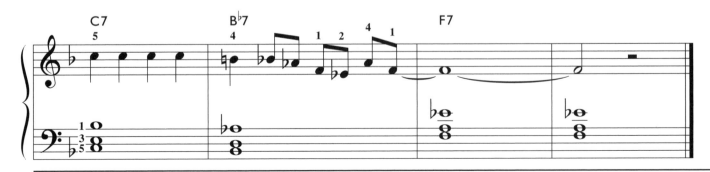

Observe what happens if we combine all the notes from the three dominant 7th chords in a C blues progression (C7—C, E, G, B♭; F7—F, A, C, E♭ and G7—G, B, D, F) and number them in relation to the key:

C	D	E♭	E	F	G	A	B♭	(B)
1	2	♭3	3	4	5	6	♭7	(7)

With the exception of B, all of these notes are found in either the C Major Pentatonic scale (C, D, E, G, A) or the C Minor Pentatonic scale (C, E♭, F, G, B♭).

> Blues melodies sound great with notes from both the major and minor pentatonic scales combined.

As you play through *Everything Blues*, notice which notes are from the major pentatonic scale and which are from the minor pentatonic scale.

 *EVERYTHING BLUES*

Track 19

TENSION AND RESOLUTION

In *Everything Blues* (page 39), you played nearly the same melody in the fifth bar as in the first, but the E natural was missing from the fifth bar. In its place is the note E♭. It sounds natural because the harmony changed from the I chord to the IV chord. The IV chord is F7, and the ♭7 of F7 is E♭. If we played an E natural over the F7 chord it would sound quite dissonant. (Try it. The E clashes with E♭ and with F.) So, we change our melody to fit the chord. This is one way in which we control the amount of tension in our melodies.

Go through the C blues progression one chord at a time. Over each chord, play the notes of the C Major Pentatonic and then the C Blues scale. First, determine which notes sound tense and which sound resolved over C7. Write your observations on a piece of scrap paper. Now do the same thing for F7. Do the same for G7. As you might have guessed, some notes that sound tense over C7 sound resolved over F7 and G7 and vice-versa.

And then there's the mighty ♭5. It sounds tense over *all* the chords. That's why it's the spiciest of all the blue notes. Usually we pass through it on the way up to the 5th or on our way down towards the root.

Here again are the notes from both the major and minor pentatonic scales combined:

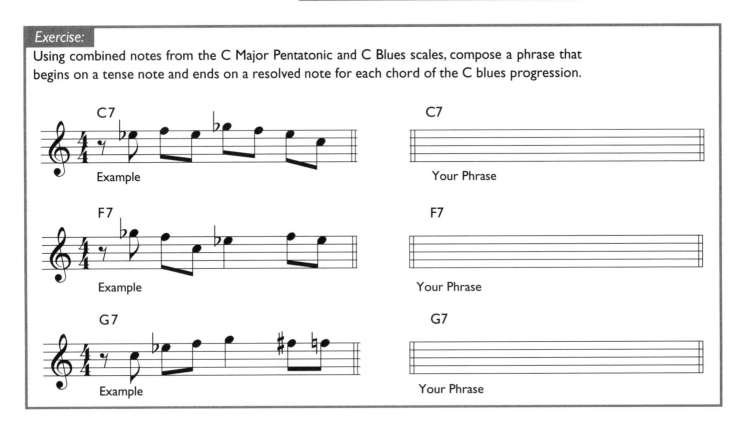

It is probably most difficult to write a phrase that sounds resolved over the V chord—in this case, G7. The V chord functions as the climax, or most unresolved point, in the chord progression. Because we are accustomed to harmonies that move in a cycle of 5ths, our ears want to hear the V chord resolve to I. We don't hear a resolution until we leave the V chord.

Once again, it's time for you to be the composer and experiment with creating blues melodies. In *C Blues*, there is an accompaniment provided. If you have the CD that is available for this book, you'll be able to practice playing your own blues along with a rhythm section!

Remember, we have talked about three different scales that you can use:

major pentatonic

minor pentatonic

blues scale

*Choosing notes from just one scale can be as effective as
using notes from combined scales. Let your ear be your guide.*

Here are a few other things to think about:

- Imagine that there are lyrics. You are telling a story, so remember to speak in clear sentences.
- Tension is ok. Just be sure to follow it with some resolution.
- Repetition and call and response are integral parts of the blues.
- Less is more. Space between phrases makes them stronger.

C BLUES
Track 20

CHAPTER 4

Playing a Shuffle

We already know from learning a shuffle-style bass line (page 24) that a shuffle is played with a triplet, or $\frac{12}{8}$ feeling, also called swing eighths. But there's a whole lot more to learn about the art of playing a shuffle. The shuffle has been developing for nearly a century now, with each great blues player along the way adding their signature to its evolution. In addition to the characteristic feel and bass patterns of shuffles, there are stylistic elements like *breaks*, *fills* and particular sounds that make a tune sound like a shuffle. You might hear a classic shuffle referred to also as a Chicago-style blues, because Chicago was the city where the great players played when the style was developing.

As a blues pianist, you get to play lots of different roles. You can be melodic, harmonic or rhythmic—or some combination of all three. When you play a solo shuffle on the piano, you actually fill many roles at once: you tell the story, you propel it forward with rhythm and you punctuate it. When you play with a singer or a band, you'll be trading roles with the other musicians, and will need to always find a niche to play in that will enhance the music. As you learn to play the blues, listen to both solo piano players and pianists with bands. Listen to how the piano player's role changes from situation to situation, and from moment to moment, within one song. That way, as you acquire more skills on the keyboard, you will be ready to use them musically.

In this chapter, we'll learn about the feeling of a shuffle, about when and how to fill up the spaces in a melody and about putting the icing on top of whatever else might be going on without getting in its way.

PHOTO • BILL GREENSMITH

Eddie Boyd, *was very active in the Chicago scene during the 1940s and '50s. Known for the sophistication of his playing, Eddie Boyd played briefly with Muddy Waters. He then went on to play with Sonny Boy Williamson's band. Boyd provided excellent accompaniment to Johnny Shines and Jimmy Rogers as well as recording his own tunes. His biggest hit was* Five Long Years *(J.O.B. Records) which topped the R&B charts in 1952.*

Here's a shuffle in F using another type of shuffle bassline. First, play the left hand alone and remember to swing the eighth notes. In your right hand, you'll be adding triplets. Since the bassline is swung, your left and right hands will play together on the first and third part of each triplet.

CHICAGO TIME

Track 21

Exercise:
- Go through this blues and notice where the ♭5 (C♭ or B♮) is being played. Play each phrase with a ♭5 in it a few times to get familiar with how it is used.
- Transpose this bassline into the key of C. It's easy, because the bassline outlines each chord the same way: R, 3, 5, 6, ♭7.

FUN WITH THE ♭5

In bars 9 and 10 of *Chicago Time* you played a figure that is very common in the blues: the ♭5, resolving to the 5. This figure sounds even better when you add the root on top.

Your right handthumb and second finger will alternate between the ♭5 and 5, while your pinkie repeats the root on top. Try it slowly.

Now play the exercise again, but move your right hand up one octave.

Sometimes your favorite blues licks will sound better in the higher ranges of the piano. If, for example, you play with guitar players, most of the guitar notes will be in a relatively low range. If you play figures in the low to middle range of the piano (around middle C) while the guitar player is in the same range, your sound will get lost, or it will add too much clutter to the sound. There will be too much going on in one range. But, if in the same situation, you play in the upper range of the keyboard, your sound will come through on the top. Of course, the guitar player might not like you playing something above what they are doing, but sometimes it's very effective. Use discretion. Listen to great players and then trust your ears.

Learn to find this common lick quickly and easily in all twelve keys. Here is an exercise taking it through four keys starting with E (a favorite key of guitar players). Continue through the cycle of 5ths.

Practice slowly and stop if you feel fatigued. It takes a little patience to get used to playing these repetitive figures smoothly.

We've learned two basslines that work for shuffles:

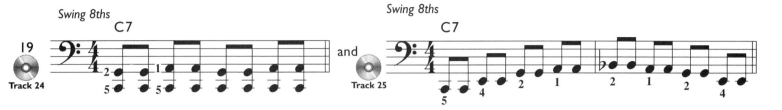

They have a few things in common: they are made up of swing eighths; they start on the root; and they outline the chords somehow. Notice that the 6th keeps showing up in these lines. You can think of the 6th in a couple of different ways. In the first pattern, it's substituting for the 7th. Using the 6 instead of the $\flat$7 gives the chord a more open sound— not specifically dominant. In the second example, the 6th is used as a passing tone on the way to the $\flat$7.

Here are a few more typical shuffle basslines:

> *Exercise:*
> Choose one of the basslines above and take it through a twelve-bar blues progression in the key of F.

The bass player in a blues band will sometimes play just the root of the chord on each beat of the bar, or in the swing eighth rhythm. In that case, it might be your role, or the guitar players role, to play one of the these shuffle patterns above the bass. Again, you have to use your ears to hear what works.

Flat Five Shuffle gives you some more practice with your new ♭5 lick, as well as a new bass line pattern.

FLAT FIVE SHUFFLE
Track 29

Observe what's happening in the last bar. That little musical figure, and the G7 chord, is called a *turnaround*. A turnaround brings you back to the beginning of the form so you can play another *chorus* (once through the form is usually referred to as one chorus). We'll learn more about turnarounds a little later in this book.

TREMOLOS AND FILLS

You've heard them—maybe you've already played them. If you haven't, you undoubtedly want to. *Tremolos* in the right hand, over a nice shuffle groove, are an essential ingredient in the blues sound. A tremolo is a rapid alternation between two notes. Sometimes blues players will call this a *roll*.

There are a few different notes you can tremolo between that sound great. We'll start with the most obvious: **the root.**

You can tremolo between the root and the ♭3 of the key over almost the whole blues progession.

In the key of F: Put your thumb on F, and your 2nd or 3rd finger on A♭. Now roll your hand back and forth between the two notes. It might seem awkward at first, but it will become more natural as you keep working at it. The key is to keep your hand relaxed. If this technique is new to you, be careful not to overdo it in the beginning. It is better to practice new techniques for a few moments frequently, rather than trying to sit down and master something all at once.

This is how tremolos or rolled notes are notated in the written music:

Tremolo on F and A♭ for 5 beats.

The next song will help you develop this new technique.

TREMS AND FILLS

Notice what happened in bar 9. That little F♯ is an enharmonic respelling of the ♭5 (G♭) in the key of C, which is the chord you are playing over in that bar. Play the F♯ quickly with the C and slide to the G, the 5 in the key of C. Some people call this a *crush tone* or a *grace note*. We'll do more of this in the next few chapters.

CHAPTER 5

Piano Blues Sounds

The piano can be the most exciting instrument to play, as well as the most challenging, because it can be so many things. It's a melodic instrument, a harmonic instrument and a percussion instrument all rolled into one. In no style of music is this more evident than the blues. As we further explore the art of blues piano, it will become more difficult to draw clear lines between what's the melody, what's the harmony and what's adding to the groove. It will become important to think in terms of "piano blues sounds" and develop a whole vocabulary of sounds that you can put together in order to get just the right feeling.

PHOTO • COURTESY OF THE INSTITUTE OF JAZZ STUDIES

Otis Spann is considered by many to be the greatest blues ensemble pianist ever. In 1952 Otis Spann was introduced to Muddy Waters by Len Chess, and joined Muddy in what would become a history-making band. Spann's solid, powerful playing style was derived in large part from Maceo Merriweather, who was on the Chicago scene before him. But Otis's unique contribution to the art was in finding the perfect way to make his bold sounds enhance but never intrude upon the new sounds of the Chicago blues.

We learned a bit about classic blues sounds, such as the ♭3 tremolo and the ♭5 lick, in Chapter 4. In this chapter, we'll focus on more piano blues sounds and how to use them. There is perhaps no one better to inspire an appetite for these sounds than Otis Spann. Listen to nearly any Otis Spann cut and you will hear wrenching blue-note clusters, driving trills and cascading blues riffs explode from his piano. He uses the piano to help tell a story, which is what the blues is all about.

In the pre-electric and early electric days of the blues, pianists like Otis Spann were playing unamplified pianos in noisy clubs and had to find ways of being heard. This led to the development of techniques to make big sounds. Licks were frequently played in the high ranges of the piano, notes were tremoloed or played in octaves and dissonant *clusters* (groups of notes a major or minor 2nd apart played simultaneously) were barked out in the guitar breaks. These sounds are still an integral part of playing the style. A good blues keyboardist needs to know exactly how and when to use them in order to enhance the music.

OTIS'S BLUES

Track 31

The most important part of learning the blues is listening. It's time for you to start shopping around for your own favorite sounds on recordings. Listen to Otis Spann solo or with Muddy Waters' incredible band. Check out Maceo Merriweather, Lafayette Leake, Memphis Slim, Meade Lux Lewis and Jimmy Yancey. Stop your recording at the spot that grabs you the most and see if you can figure out what sound the piano player is playing. If you don't already have many blues recordings, there are some great blues piano compilations available which will give you a sampling (see the discography in the back of this book). You can also find classic blues recordings in your library.

THREE-NOTE ♭5 LICK

Let's take a look at what you were playing when you played *Otis's Blues* on page 49. The first line starts out with a classic Otis Spann sound played as a cluster. The notes are A♯, B and D. In relation to the key of E, these are the ♭5, the 5 and the ♭7—three notes out of the E Blues scale. In the first two bars they're played as a cluster, and in the third bar they are arpeggiated, which we know means played one at a time. Both of these ways of playing the ♭5, 5 and ♭7 sound great over the blues progression in any key. You should know where these notes are in every key and be able to grab them quickly.

Exercise:

Play the following four-bar figure in all twelve keys, moving through the keys in ascending 4ths (or downward 5ths). In your left hand, play the first basic shuffle pattern we learned. In your right hand play the ♭5, 5 and ♭7 for that key. Experiment with playing the notes individually, as a repeated cluster, or try trilling them. Here are a few keys to get you started:

FOUR-NOTE ♭5 LICK

In the tenth bar of *Otis's Blues*, you played what might be the most well-known of all blues piano licks. For this lick, we use the first four notes of the blues scale: the root, the ♭3, 4 and ♭5. This lick is almost always played using sixteenth notes (or notes with an even shorter rhythmic value.)

Let's learn this lick using sixteenth notes. This means there are four notes for every beat. Even though we are swinging the eighth notes when we play a shuffle, we will give each sixteenth note equal rhythmic value. Try playing this lick in the key of E, to a metronome set at 60.

When you can play it smoothly, turn the metronome faster a few clicks at a time, playing the lick at each new tempo. When you are comfortable at 80 or 90 beats per minute, try adding the shuffle pattern in your left hand. Remember to keep the swing feel in your left hand, but try to play all the sixteenth notes equally in your right hand. Practicing each hand separately with a metronome until it is very comfortable will help you to put the two hands together.

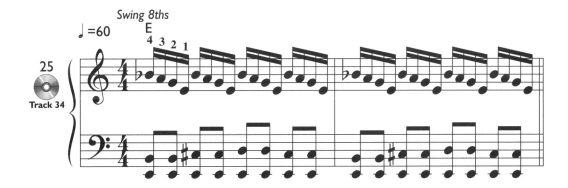

Exercise:

In the keys of E and A, play your new blues lick through the entire blues progression using sixteenth notes in your right hand and any of the shuffle patterns we've learned in your left hand. Although you might want to play the right-hand lick even faster (in other words, with notes shorter than sixteenth notes), keep it to sixteenth notes at first. It is important to learn to play different rhythmic patterns with control (confidence and accuracy). The cool rhythmic stuff you'll want to play down the road will only sound cool if you learn habits of control now.

Blues pianists use *octave doublings* for volume and dramatic effect. For a great example of this, listen to Chicago Pianist Lafayette Leake playing behind Howlin' Wolf on the tune *Louise* (Chess Records). The descending octaves on the piano becomes an integral part of the arrangement.

If you have not worked a lot on piano technique, or tried to play octaves before, they might seem difficult at first. As with any new technique, it's important to start slowly and stay relaxed.

Let's begin in E, by playing the root in octaves:

Now try this simple lick from the blues scale:

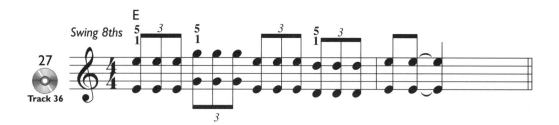

Once the exercises above are comfortable, try playing the whole blues scale in octaves.

Ascending...

...and descending.

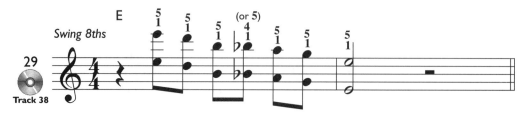

*Undersung pianist
Lafayette Leake played
with a host of Chicago
blues guitarists and
vocalists in the 1950s
and '60s including Otis
Rush's and Muddy
Water's main rival for
attention on the
Chicago scene, Howlin'
Wolf (Chester Burnett).*

LAFAYETTE'S BLUES
Track 39

Major "Big Maceo" Merriweather came up during the boogie-woogie craze, and went on to become one of the most popular blues artists on the Chicago scene in the 1940s. Maceo's piano style was hugely influential to the young pianists coming up in Chicago, most notably two of Muddy Waters' pianists: Little Johnny Jones and Otis Spann.

Maceo sang and played, and his songs were mainly his own, many of them in the sixteen-bar blues form. His most well-known song is Worried Life Blues, *which borrowed a verse from guitarist Sleepy John Estes. Maceo's first recording session took place in 1941, and unfortunately his last was in 1945. Shortly after that time, Maceo suffered a paralyzing stroke, and though he recovered from it, he never again reached the place in his playing that he left. The 1945 session produced Maceo's solo masterpiece,* Chicago Breakdown, *a classic example of boogie-woogie piano at its finest.*

CHICAGO PIANO SOUNDS ON THE MINOR BLUES

Frequently, a minor blues will be a funky or jazzy blues, with a whole different feel from a shuffle or delta blues. There are blues tunes, however, that sound similar to *Otis's Blues* (page 49), except that the i chord is minor. In these cases the form is usually i, IV, V. For example, in the key of F, the chords in the progression would be Fmin, B♭7 and C7. Since the sounds we've been working on in this chapter come from the blues scale, which is mainly the minor pentatonic, they'll work fine over a blues with a i, IV7, V7 progression. Below is an example of a minor blues shuffle. It includes sounds you know, but puts them into a slightly different context.

This blues is in the style of a very successful tune that left-handed guitarist and vocalist Otis Rush recorded for Chess Records called *So Many Roads*.

> *A *pickup* is a note (or notes) that occur before the first full measure of a piece.

RUSH'S ROADS

Track 40

PLAYING OFF OF TRIADS

In Chapter 3, you learned that we can alter blues melodies to fit the chords as they change (page 40). Let's take that concept one step further and consider playing deliberately "off of" each chord.

Here is a way of playing off of triads that might be the most frequently played keyboard sound in popular music:

If you wanted to analyze it harmonically, you could say it's a quick I-IV-I progression with the IV chord in second inversion, and the I chord in root position (see the triads review on page 15, and the section on triad inversions on page 22). Every chord in the blues is then treated as a I-IV-I. Alternatively, you could just think of it as tension-resolution—moving away from the chord tones and then coming back.

BENDING THE 3RD

When we play these figures off of triads, it's nice to add the ♭3 as a *grace note* preceding the 3rd. A grace note is a quick ornamental note played directly before the main note. Some of us call this *bending the 3rd* because it sounds similar to a guitar player bending a note. It feels more natural in some keys than in others, depending upon where the black notes and white notes fall under your fingers. Here's how it works:

If the ♭3 is a black note, and the 3 is a white note, as in the keys of C, F or G, you can simply slide your 2nd finger from the ♭3 to the 3.

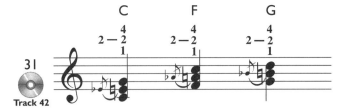

If the ♭3 is a white note, and the 3 is a black note, it's a little more awkward. Try playing the ♭3 with your 2nd finger and the 3 with your 3rd finger.

You'll find that you gravitate to certain sounds in certain keys, and each key will have its own vocabulary for that reason. It's a good idea, however, to practice each new sound in all twelve keys. It helps you to learn the sound really well—and sometimes you will have to play in G♭ on a gig!

Triad Blues gives you some practice with the device you just learned. Although it is not indicated in the music, go ahead and try bending the 3rd of each chord. In this case, all the ♭3s are black notes and all the 3s are white notes, so you can slide your 2nd finger from ♭3 to 3.

TRIAD BLUES
Track 44

Exercise:

Try to play through *Triad Blues* in the key of F. The I will be F, the IV will be B♭ and the V will be C. Bending the 3rd for the IV (B♭) chord is a little trickier than it was in C (where the IV is F). All the notes will be a perfect 4th higher. Try it, but remember, bending notes is an aesthetic choice. You don't need to do it all the time. Sometimes, you might want to just play the chord cleanly.

In the same way that we played off of triads, we can play figures off of dominant 7th chords.

Let's look again at the figure you just played off of a triad:

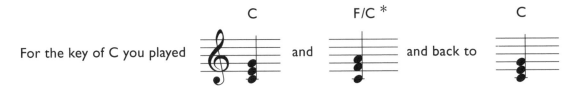

For the key of C you played   and   and back to

Instead of returning to the triad (C, E and G), move the note F up a whole step to G and the note A up a half step to B♭. You are playing the root, 5th and ♭7th of a C7 chord.

Try playing this sequence that starts from the top and goes down:

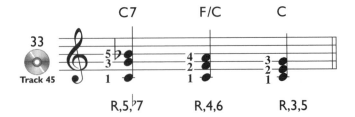

> * This is called a *slash chord*. The letter to the left of the slash is the name of the chord. The letter to the right of the chord is the name of the note on the bottom. This is a convenient way to indicate a chord inversion, or the presence of a non-chord tone in the bass.

Now try the same thing starting with a G7 chord:

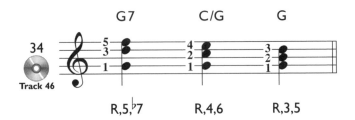

With a D7 chord, let's start from the triad and go up to the dominant 7th chord:

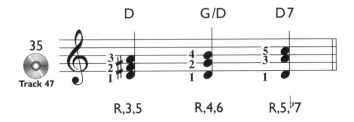

Dominant Blues will give you some practice with playing off the dominant 7th chords.

DOMINANT BLUES

Track 48

Exercise:

From the following list of new concepts and sounds from this chapter and Chapter 4, choose three devices and incorporate them into your own piano blues:

Three-note ♭5 lick   Octave doublings
Four-note ♭5 lick   Playing off of triads
♭5 lick with root on top   Playing off of dominant chords
Tremolos   Triplets

CHAPTER 6

A Look at Boogie-Woogie

Boogie-woogie piano was one of the earliest blues piano styles to develop. It was the result of the combined influences of ragtime piano and "barrelhouse" playing (a rougher or cruder version of ragtime which featured heavy left-hand playing known as stomping). Boogie-woogie was characterized by forceful left-hand bass figures which featured repetitive and often fast eight-to-the bar rhythms (a feel in which all the eighth notes are given equal weight). Volume and momentum are important aspects of boogie-woogie playing, and it is perhaps for this reason that bass lines with octave doublings frequently appeared. Many historians think boogie-woogie emerged from the South, as did Clarence "Pine Top" Smith who made the boogie style famous with his 1928 recording of *Pine Top's Boogie-Woogie* for Vocalian records. The boogie-woogie craze subsided by the 1950s as electric blues bands like Muddy Waters' changed the sound of the blues. But the influence of boogie-woogie piano on the blues continued to be great. In 1986, boogie-woogie legend Jimmy Yancey was inducted into the Rock and Roll Hall of Fame as the one who "gave rock its roll."

Boogie Blues on page 61 is a boogie-woogie tune in C. The feel is a little different from a shuffle. The tempo is faster than the shuffles you have been playing, and the eighth notes are not swung as hard. In other words, the eighth notes will become closer to straight eighths. Remember that straight eighths get equal rhythmic value, while in swing eighths the first of each pair is held longer than the second.

Practice this tune slowly with a metronome, then increase the tempo a click or two at a time until it is up to the metronome marking.

> ### Clarence "Pine Top" Smith
> *might be considered the father of boogie-woogie. His influence gave rise to pianists like Jimmy Yancey, Meade Lux Lewis, Albert Ammons, Charles "Cow-Cow" Davenport and Pete Johnson.* Pine Top's Boogie Woogie, *one of the most influential blues recordings of all time, was a dance piece. Pine Top himself was an all-around entertainer who sang and tap danced in addition to playing the piano. His recording days were short-lived—at age twenty-five he was accidentally shot during a dispute in the Masonic lodge where he was playing.*

BOOGIE BLUES

Track 49

Almost Straight 8ths

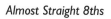

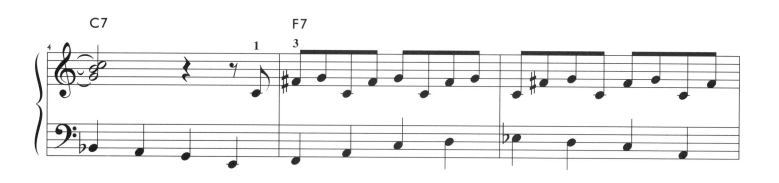

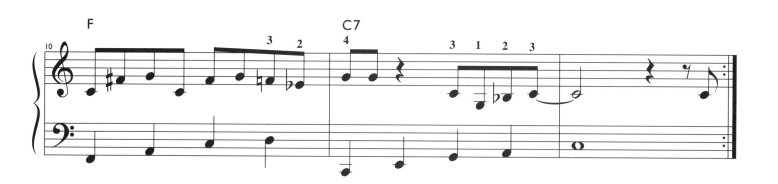

Let's review eighth-note feels, using the melody from *Boogie Blues*.

You'll play the first line of the melody three times with your metronome set to 80.

The first time, play the eighth notes straight:

The second time, play the line as you did for a shuffle—swinging the eighth notes in a triplet feel:

The third time, try to play the melody in a feel somewhere between straight eighths and triplet feel. Think about making the first note of each pair just a little longer than the second. Don't worry if it seems difficult, at this point you are just trying to increase your understanding of the different feels.

BOOGIE-WOOGIE BASS LINES

A boogie-woogie bass line has either four or eight notes per bar. It either outlines the chords or "walks." In either case it might contain repeated notes, or notes repeated an octave away.

Look at the bass line you just played for *Boogie Blues* (page 61). The notes are similar to other bass lines you have played, but the feel is different. For a shuffle, your left hand plays eighth notes with a triplet feel, while your right hand either played triplets, or swung the eighths along with your left. In this boogie bass line, you play quarter notes instead of eighth notes. That leaves the right hand free to play the eighths note a little more evenly. At quicker tempos, the eighth notes will sound almost straight.

To make this bass line into an eighth-note line in a boogie style, we could add octaves:

WALKING THE BASS

Walking the bass means that instead of just playing chord tones in the bass line, you connect the chord tones with scale tones, taking smaller steps between notes. You "walk" up the scale from which the chord is built.

Here is *Boogie Blues* again with a simple walking bass line. For each chord, the bass line uses the first three notes of the scale that the chord is taken from.

WALKING BOOGIE BLUES

We can make our walking boogie bass line an eighth-note line, by adding octaves:

> **Exercise:**
> Play through *Walking Boogie Blues* one more time using the walking line with octaves.

Just as for other blues styles, boogie-woogie can be in a major or minor key. Here is a minor boogie that uses the same type of walking bass line you just played. Since the chords are minor, the notes in the bass line come from a minor scale.

This tune uses minor 7th chords (min7). To make a minor 7th chord, take the formula for a dominant 7th chord (1, 3, 5, $\flat$7) and flat the 3rd (1, $\flat$3, 5, $\flat$7).

1	$\flat$3	5	$\flat$7
C	E$\flat$	5	$\flat$7

This is a Cmin7 chord.

Cmin7

SO LONG BOOGIE

Track 55

We could also turn this walking boogie line upside down, walking down from the root rather than up. Let's keep the octaves. The chords are min7 chords, so the next note down from the root will be a whole step below the root (the $\flat$7).

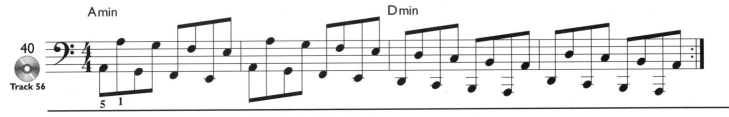

In *Boogie Train*, your right hand provides some forward momentum. Right-hand boogie parts were often simple and repetitive. The most important part of boogie-woogie is always the rhythm. Play just the right hand part to *Boogie Train* several times, then add the left hand. Play the eighth notes with an almost straight feel.

BOOGIE TRAIN

Track 57

JIMMY YANCEY-STYLE BOOGIE-WOOGIE

The right-hand part you played in *Boogie Train* is similar to what Jimmy Yancey might have played on a boogie tune. However, now that you've gotten used to thinking about playing the eighths straighter, we are going to complicate things by playing a Jimmy Yancey style of boogie which, like a shuffle, is played in a triplet feel!

Try the bass line alone first:

The right-hand part is the same as what you played for *Boogie Train*, with some *leading tones* added. Leading tones are notes in a melody or bass line that don't necessarily come from the chord or the scale from which the chord is built, but are used to approach a chord tone. This relates to issues of tension and resolution discussed in Chapter 3. Leading tones are a half-step above or below chord tones and always resolve to chord tones.

It's time to put the two parts together.

JIMMY'S BOOGIE
Track 60

James Edward "Jimmy" Yancey is thought by many to be the master of boogie-woogie, but his quiet stage demeanor did not lend itself to stardom, and he did not tour or record as prolifically as his own protogées. On the bandstand, Jimmy frequently provided accompaniment to his wife, a vocalist, Estelle "Mama" Yancey. Despite Jimmy Yancey's subdued nature, his music was part of the boogie-woogie craze. Jimmy Yancey is respected by both blues and jazz enthusiasts as a master of his art.

CHAPTER 7

Rhythm, Comping, Playing in a Band

Piano players such as Otis Spann and Pinetop Perkins, who played with Muddy Waters, came up with the perfect piano parts to accentuate the groove, support or punctuate a solo or just enhance the overall sound. When you play blues piano with a band, you will have to do the same. You will be faced with certain aesthetic choices, and will need a varied palette of rhythmic, harmonic and melodic tools to draw from in order to make good choices.

PHOTO • COURTESY OF STARFILES, INC.

Muddy Waters, the King of the Chicago blues scene in the 1950s, surrounded himself with extraordinary musicians. He put together history-making bands with vocals, guitar, harmonica, piano, bass and drums. Muddy's bands played a blues style that was firmly based in country blues, but the originality and sophistication of their sound, and their arrangements, moved the style significantly forward.

COMPING

Comping is a word that comes from the word "accompaniment." Musicians use "comping" as a catch-all term for what piano players or guitar players play behind a soloist. Basically, to *comp* is to play the chords.

When comping, you deal with three elements of music: rhythm, harmony and melody. Over the next few pages, we will deal with knowing what chords to play (harmony), having control over where you want to put them in the time (rhythm) and making the chord motion sound good (melody). If you master your comping skills, you will make the band sound great and be in demand!

Let's start with a simple comping exercise using triads. Your left hand plays on the first and third beats of each bar, while your right hand plays on two and four.

BLUES IN G

Track 61

Exercise:

Transpose the above exercise into the key of F. Determine the inversions used for the I, IV and V chords.

VOICE LEADING

The triads in the *Blues in G* (page 69) were in certain inversions to create good voice leading. Notice how the top note stayed the same when you moved from the I chord to the IV chord (measure 4 and 5). Also, the top note of your voicings for the whole first eight bars was the root of the key. You can almost never go wrong with the root as the top note of your chord. Keeping this idea in mind will help you play more complex chords and progressions.

In *Comping in D*, you will use the same pattern of inverted triads, but your right hand will play a dotted-quarter rhythm (see page 20).

COMPING IN D
Track 62

Now that you're comfortable with that rhythm, we're going to make the left hand work a little harder. Your left hand is going to play the first shuffle pattern you learned (page24). Swing the eighths. Instead of just counting the beats, think about playing the shuffle patter in your left hand and then adding your right. Your hands should line up on the first beat of every bar and the "and of 2" of every bar. Another way to think of it is that your right hand plays the second chord of each bar together with the fourth note of your left hand.

COMPING SHUFFLE IN D

Track 63

> **Exercise:**
>
> Let's assume that our shuffle just became an uptempo boogie-woogie or rock-and-roll tune. Play through the same exercise again, exactly as written, but play the eighth notes almost straight with the metronome set at 120.

THE BEAUTY OF FILLS

When you listen to a great blues singer sing or guitarist play, they always leave space between phrases. A great blues band does brilliant things with that space. This is where *fills* come in. The fills in a blues tune can be almost as important as the phrases they fall between. Think of fills as being affirmation and punctuation of what the soloist is saying.

Johnnie Jones played with a great Chicago guitarist/vocalist named Elmore James. James played a song called *Dust My Broom*. The way the fills fell in that song became a format upon which many blues tunes were based. Listen to *Dust My Broom* to get a good feeling for the interplay between voice, guitar and band.

Here is a twelve-bar blues showing where fills might typically fall in a *Dust My Broom* style shuffle.

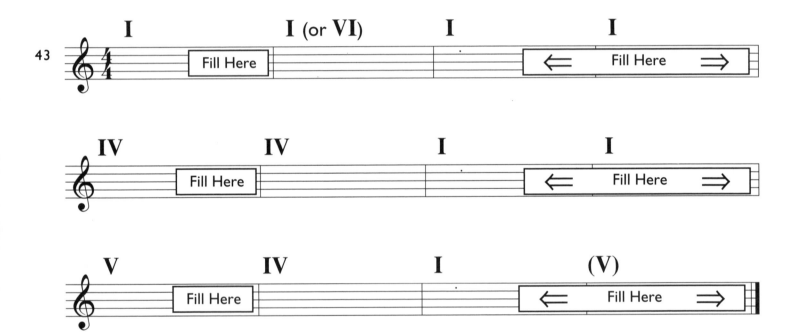

If you are playing behind a vocalist and there is no guitar, then it might be up to you to provide all the right fills. If there's a guitar player, you have to be ready to react with just the right commentary to everything they play or don't play. Your fills can be made up of all the different piano blues sounds we've talked about—trills, clusters, ♭5 licks, etc.

Guitar Player is a shuffle in C. There is a melody part written for guitar (in small, cue-sized notes) so that you get a chance to be the fill-master. If you have the CD that is available for this book, you can play along with it. Otherwise it might be time for you to start hanging out with some fellow blues players and working on these concepts together. Communication with other musicians is the most important musical skill you can have.

GUITAR PLAYER

Track 64

COMPING WITH OCTAVES

You don't always have to play all of the notes in the chords. In fact, if someone else is already comping, or playing a very dense solo right in the midrange (like a guitar player) you could choose to lay out completely, or play something with a more open sound.

One way to add to the groove without cluttering the sonic space is to play a repeated rhythmic figure in octaves.

In *Octavia,* your right hand plays a rhythm that is typical of what a horn section might play. Again, you will have to subdivide to eighth notes to count the rhythm. Make sure to note the beats on which your right hand plays.

Track 65

DOMINANT 7TH CHORD INVERSIONS

Since much of blues harmony is based on the sound of dominant 7th chords, it's important to be very familiar with them in every key. Good voice leading is something you'll always want to strive for, and that means you need to be able to easily invert dominant 7th chords.

Since dominant 7th chords have four notes, they have four positions.

Let's look at a C7 chord:

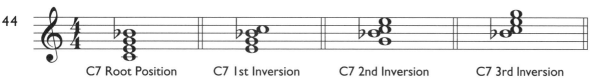

Play through the following exercise to familiarize yourself with all the dominant 7th chord positions in all keys. Something to notice: with the exception of root position, you will always have a whole step between the dominant 7th and the root in your voicing. Try it with your left hand, too.

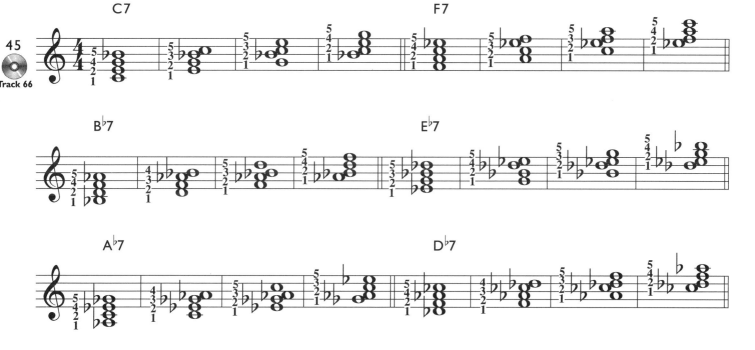

Now continue down through the second half of the cycle of 5ths. Don't forget, guitar players like to play in sharp keys like A and E, so don't ignore them!

Now we can use inverted dominant 7th chords to comp through a blues in G, using a classic rhythm that will work over a swing or straight eighth feel. Because we know it sounds good, we'll start with the root (G), as the top note of the chord.

There's no left hand part written here. Sometimes, when you're comping in a band, it sounds too cluttered if you play with both hands. Focus only on your right hand for a few times then, if you wish, try it together with a simple left hand shuffle pattern.

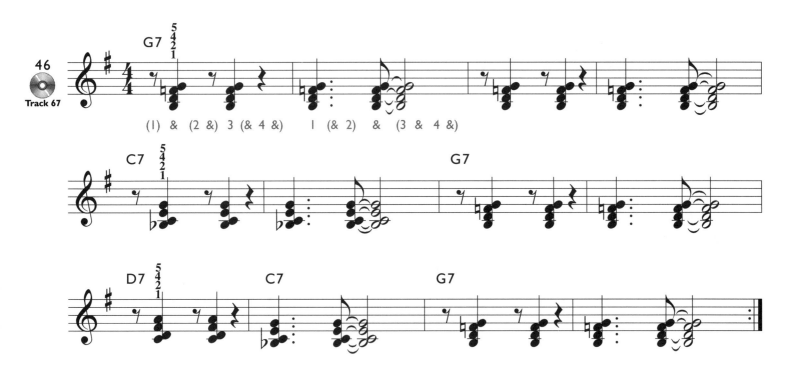

Exercise:

Let's try putting the 5th in the top voice of the first chord. The 5th of G7 is D, so our first chord would be G7 in 3rd inversion. When you move to the C7, your top note has to change, because there is no D in C7. Try to make it change as little as possible, making a melodic move rather than a big leap. There are two notes in C7 that are only a whole step from D (C and E). Pick either one and make that the top note of your C7 chord.

Experiment and discover for yourself what will happen when you get to the V chord, D7. You'll find that if you play the V in 1st inversion, the top voice will not have to move—the D is common to both chords (I and V).

The following example is a comping pattern in the style of guitarist Freddie King's classic shuffle, *Hideaway*. The example is in E, which is the key of the original song.

YOU CAN RUN BUT YOU CAN'T HIDE

Track 68

In *You Can Run but You Can't Hide*, the bass line is written out for your left hand. If you were on a gig with a bass player, the bass player would play that line, and you would not want to double it. Instead, you could either play nothing with your left hand, (usually a safe choice) or the root, 5, 6 shuffle pattern from page 24.

SCRATCH MY BACK COMP

In Chapter 5, you learned about playing off of triads. You can use this concept for comping as well. The following example is in the style of the comping pattern for the classic Slim Harpo tune, *Scratch My Back*. Notice the leading-tone on the third eighth note of each bar. The tension it causes makes this a very distinctive pattern.

PARALLEL 6THS

Now that you know dominant 7th chord inversions, we can change the triad pattern just a little bit to get another classic comping pattern that Jimmy Yancey favored called *parallel 6ths* (the interval between two notes in the pattern remains that of a 6th—hence the name).

Let's look again at the *Scratch My Back* pattern you learned in *The Blues Itch* and see how we can change a few things to get a parallel 6ths pattern:

47

Parallel Blues gives you a chance to practice the most commonly heard way of playing parallel 6ths. In this twelve-bar blues, the IV chord appears in the second bar, for just one measure. This is common in several blues styles. Next time you listen to a blues recording, listen for a "quick IV" in the second bar.

PARALLEL BLUES

Track 70

Exercise:

Transpose *Parallel Blues* into the key of D. If it seems tricky to play, start by playing a D triad and figuring out the *Scratch My Back* pattern you learned in *The Blues Itch* (page 78) in D.

MINOR 7TH CHORD INVERSIONS

As you used four-note chords to comp on a dominant 7th blues, you might want to use minor 7th chords on a minor blues. This will be the case more frequently on a funky or jazz-style blues, where the harmony is specifically based on minor 7th chords.

Let's check out minor 7th chord inversions with a Cmin7 chord:

Play through the following exercise to familiarize yourself with inversions of minor 7th chords. This time we are going around the cycle of 5ths in the opposite direction, moving up in 5ths.

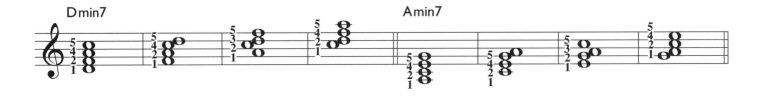

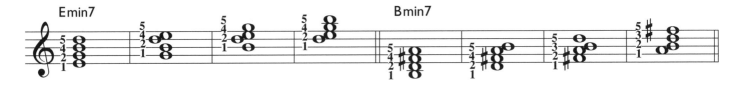

Continue up through the rest of the cycle.

The voice leading concepts you know apply when you are comping with minor 7th chords. If, for example, you wanted to start a minor blues with the root at the top of your voicing, you would use a Amin7 chord in 1st inversion:

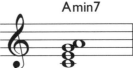

Determine which inversion of Dmin7 you would use to keep the note A as the top note of the iv chord.

Ten O'Clock Blues uses inversions of minor 7th chords. This is a funky tune with a melody, a comping pattern and a bass line pattern that introduces a new rhythm in your left hand. On the CD that is available for this book, you will hear the guitar playing the melody. For some help in coordinating the comping and bass parts, see the box at the bottom of the page.

TEN O'CLOCK BLUES

Track 73

To count the rhythms in each hand, subdivide each bar into eighth notes. Play each hand separately until you are comfortable with it.

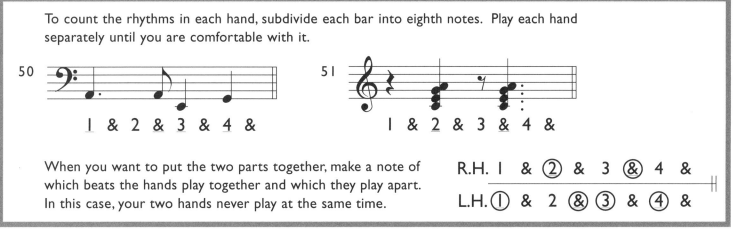

When you want to put the two parts together, make a note of which beats the hands play together and which they play apart. In this case, your two hands never play at the same time.

CHAPTER 8

Intros, Endings and Turnarounds

You've already got quite a blues stew going, but there are a few more essential ingredients needed. The time has come to address one of the most important and challenging aspects of blues playing—*turnarounds* and *endings*.

All those dominant 7th chords in the blues progression create continuous harmonic motion because they don't sound resolved. So, we need to have great, sometimes dramatic endings to wrap up the story. Turnarounds, on the other hand, add to the forward motion. As with any aspect of blues piano, there is a classic vocabulary to learn as well as room for your own design. We'll start with the basics.

TURNAROUNDS

A turnaround is a musical figure used to lead you back to the top of the form. A turnaround usually ends on a V7 chord (a *half cadence*) since the dominant V7 chord leads back to the tonic.

Some of the compositions earlier in this book included turnarounds. They included a V7 chord in the last bar of the form, and a repeat sign to indicate a return to the top of the form. Try to find them.

BASIC TURNAROUNDS

Bass walks up from the 3rd of the I chord to the root of the V chord.

Bass walks down from the ♭7 of the I chord to the root of the V chord.

We can put these two *chromatic* (using notes outside the key) approaches together with two hands.

The word "chromatic" also implies movement in half-step increments, as in the *chromatic scale* (a twelve-note scale which includes all of the white notes and all of the black notes on the piano).

To play more involved turnarounds, you need to be familiar with the neighboring chords for the key. Neighboring chords lie a half step away from the chord you are approaching. A♭7 is a neighboring chord to G7. D♭7 is a neighboring chord to C7.

Here is a basic turnaround you have already learned, but with a neighboring chord used to approach the V chord:

Play the following exercise to familiarize yourself with neighboring chords. Notice that each finger is moving only a half step. There is no need to move your hand away from the piano as you move from chord to chord. Just slide each finger to its neighboring note. Remember, all half steps on the piano are between a black note and a white note, except where the half step is between two white notes: E to F and B to C.

This exercise uses dominant 7th chords in 1st inversion. When this is mastered, try it using root position, 2nd inversion and 3rd inversion. Practice it with the left hand, too.

Example 64 is a turnaround that includes parallel 3rds in the style of Jimmy Yancey.

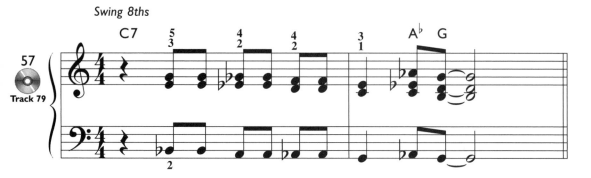

Let's take the same turnaround and make it into a triplet figure.

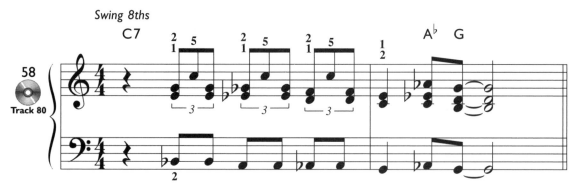

Example 66 is the "walk-up" turnaround again, but with the inner voices filled in.

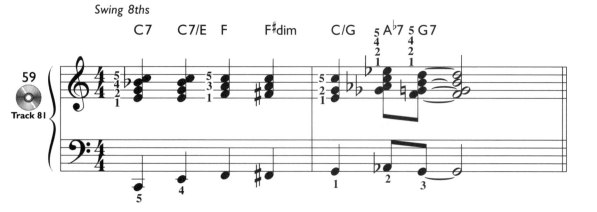

Check out the harmonic movement in this turnaround. Going from the C7 to the F is like a V7 (C7) to I (F) progression, even though this example is in C. This idea will become more important as you learn different approaches to blues playing.

Study these examples until you are comfortable enough with each turnaround to transpose it to any key.

TURNAROUND #1

TURNAROUND #2

TURNAROUND #3

Endings have the opposite function of turnarounds. Instead of taking us back to the top of the form, they take us out. Interestingly, you can transform many turnaround figures into endings just by ending on a I chord instead of the V7.

Here's a familiar turnaround transformed into an ending:

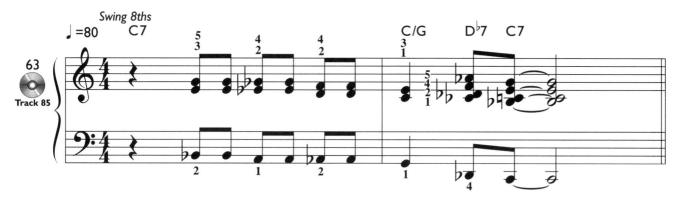

This ending approaches the I chord from below:

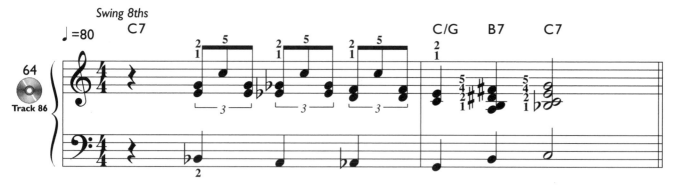

HARMONY LESSON:

Approaching a chord with its upper neighboring chord is almost the same thing as playing a V7-I7. This is because in any key, the V7 chord and the ♭II7 chord have the same 3rds and 7ths, but inverted:

In the key of C: The 3rd and 7th of G7 (V7) are B (3rd) and F (7th). The 3rd and 7th of D♭7 (♭II7) are F (3rd) and C♭, which is the enharmonic equivalent of B (7th).

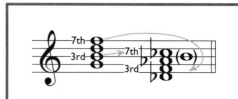

The interval between D♭ and G is called a tritone (see page 38), and **any two dominant 7th chords a tritone away from each other share the same 3rds and 7ths.**

FOLLOWING THE LEADER

Let's assume now that you're in a band, backing up a soloist (guitar player, singer, harmonica player, etc.). You'll need to listen and follow the soloist through the ending. He or she might want the band to *break* somewhere during the last few bars. During a break, everyone stops playing but the soloist. The soloist might play a fill in time or might play a *cadenza**. In the first case, you simply keep counting through the bars and play the last chord (or two chords ♭II7 to I7) at the right time. In the case of a cadenza, you need to stop playing and wait for the soloist's cue to come back in and end the tune.

> * A **cadenza** is an out-of-time solo passage, which can
> be as long or short as the soloist wishes.

If you have the CD that is available for this book, play along with this example of a shuffle ending with a break. If you don't have the CD, try this at your next jam session.

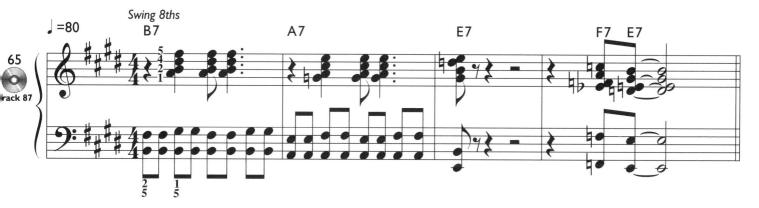

In this example, the soloist plays a cadenza on the ♭II7 and the final chord. This is shown with the *fermata* 𝄐 , or *hold* sign, over the last two chords.

INTROS

Not every blues starts with an introduction, but many of them do. As with every other aspect of the blues that we've talked about, there is some standard vocabulary to learn, as well as some room for creativity.

A common way to start a blues is to play a four-bar, V-IV-I intro with a little turnaround at the end.

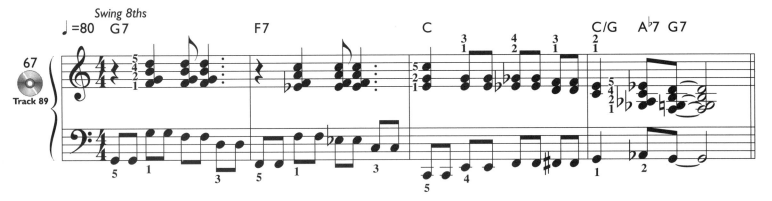

If the song you're about to play includes a riff (a short repeated figure that is the basis for the song), you or the soloist might play that riff as the intro. Notice how well the riff in bar 3 works as an intro.

Alternatively, an intro might just focus on the rhythm and set the groove.

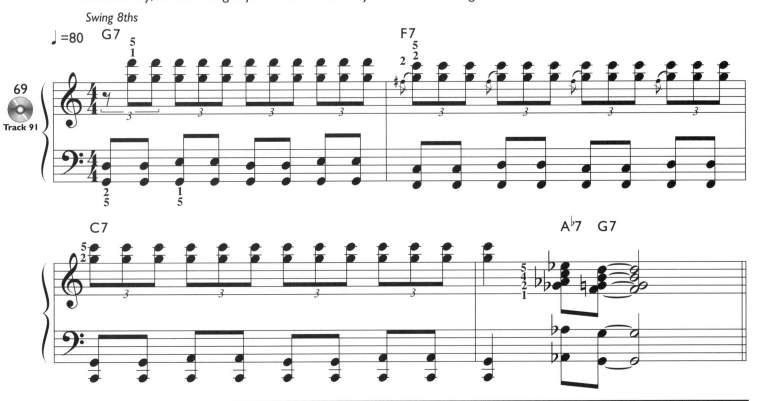

If you're playing solo piano, or you're with a band but the leader says "piano, take the intro..." then you can put any of your favorite licks or lines over the chord progression.

Track 92

Exercise:

Pick a shuffle from earlier in the book and make up two, four-bar V-IV-I intros. Let one intro have a melodic focus, and make the other as rhythmic as possible.

Producer, composer, performer **Willie Dixon** *had a career in professional boxing before pursuing a musical career. Dixon led several bands in Chicago in the 1940s. The most popular of these was The Big Three Trio, with Leonard "Baby Doo" Caston on piano—a sophisticated jump blues trio with tight arrangements by Dixon, often featuring three-part vocal harmonies. In the 1950s Willie Dixon produced sessions for Leonard Chess, wrote tunes for Chess artists like Muddy Waters, Howlin' Wolf and Little Walter and played in Muddy Waters' band. As the '50s progressed, Willie Dixon rose to greater fame and had an incredible influence on the Chicago scene. Willie Dixon claims to have written over 250 songs and has said, "I am the Blues." He certainly put his stamp firmly on blues history.*

CHAPTER 9

Walking Bass and an Introduction to The Slow Blues

In Chapter 6 you were introduced to the walking bassline. In this chapter, we will look more closely at how walking lines are constructed. As a keyboard player, you are doing one of two things: either providing a bassline or responding to one. If you are not playing the bassline because there is a bass player, you need to be hearing the bass clearly enough to make good harmonic and melodic choices. A blues with a walking bassline provides many opportunities for choices because there are many different ways to "walk" through a given set of chord changes. In addition, there will be choices about which chord changes to play, especially as you start to slow down the blues, thus stretching out the progression. Playing slow blues is a huge topic which we will begin to address here, and then flesh-out further in *Intermediate Blues Keyboard*, where we will look at more complex chord motion, basslines and voicings, how to improvise over them and how to play in the styles of several influential blues figures.

Play *Walking the Blues* slowly, paying close attention to the left hand.

WALKING THE BLUES
Track 93

BUILDING A WALKING BASSLINE

Let's look more closely at how the bassline for *Walking the Blues* is constructed:

1) Look at the first beat of each bar. In almost every measure, the root of the chord is played on the first beat. The only exceptions are bars four, eight and twelve, where the 5th of the chord is played. Notice that in each case where the 5th of the chord is played on beat one, the chord being played is the tonic I and it is being continued for a second bar. If you start your walking basslines with this kind of skeleton and fill in the blanks, you cannot go too far astray.

2) Look at the shape of the line. Most bars are either ascending (the notes all go up the staff, or descending (the notes all go down). Whether a measure is ascending or descending depends upon which octave you choose for each root when you outline the root motion. There are no hard-and-fast rules about whether you should walk up or down from one root to the next. In the first bar of *Walking the Blues*, the bass might have walked from C down to F rather than up. As always, let your ear guide you.

3) The notes you play on beats two, three and four of each bar connect the roots(or 5ths). Most of these notes come from the scale of the chord. Others are leading or *passing tones* which are outside the scale but help to connect things smoothly. Since you are walking, you will generally take small steps rather than large leaps. However, the most important thing is to make the chord changes clear and the line sound good, so there will always be some exceptions.

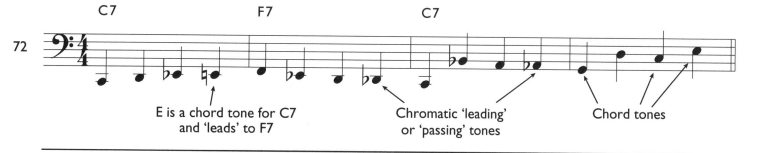

There are many ways to get from C7 (I) to F7 (IV) in four beats:

In *Walking the Blues* we walked up. We used some chromatic tones because otherwise we would have gotten to F too quickly.

An alternative might be to break up the ascending pattern, but stick to tones that are within the scale of the C7 chord(F Major).

Another way to get from C to F is to walk down.

In the twelve-bar progression, there are three times we stay on C7 for two bars. That means eight beats of C7 leading to either F7, G7 or a turnaround.

In *Walking the Blues,* we played the 5th of the chord on beat one of the second bar, but it would be OK to play the root (C) again.

You can change the direction of your walking line whenever you want. You can also put a large interval leap in wherever it seems right. The fourth bar of *Walking the Blues* doesn't walk in just one direction, but it does its job because it outlines a C7 chord and it leads to the F7 chord with the note E.

Look again at the bassline for *Walking the Blues.* This time, notice how beat four of each bar leads to beat one of the following bar. Most of the time, but not always, it will sound good to approach a root from a half-step away. Don't think of it as a rule to follow. The only rule is to make it sound good.

PRACTICE MAKING BASS LINES

Here's your chance to create some bass lines. Fill in the gaps (marked with boxes) in the bass lines below. In the second example there is a melody. Make sure your bass line doesn't clash with it—stay out of its range and make sure any dissonances make sense. Let's stick to quarter notes.

ii - V - I

In Chapter 1, you studied diatonic triads (page 15). As you learned then, the ii chord is minor. That is why it is shown with a lower case Roman numeral. The ii-V-I chord progression is commonly used in a slow blues to substitute for the V-IV-I that normally makes up the last four bars of a twelve-bar blues. In the key of C, this progression would be Dmin7 - G7 - C.

The bass walks easily through this progression.

Sad and Lonely Blues is a slow blues in G using a ii-V-I (Amin7, D7, G7) turnaround.

SAD AND LONELY BLUES

DISCOGRAPHY

Atlantic Blues	Four-CD set including blues piano compilation with Jimmy Yancey, Professor Longhair, Meade Lux Lewis, etc. There is also great piano playing on the vocal and guitar compilations. (Atlantic Records)
Blues by Roosevelt Sykes	Roosevelt Sykes. (Smithsonian Folkways)
Blues Essentials	Compilation with Muddy Waters, Elmore James, Memphis Slim, Howlin Wolf, etc. (Capitol Records)
Birth of Soul	Ray Charles. (Atlantic Records)
Boogie Woogie, Stride and Piano Blues	With Pete Johnson, James P. Johnson, etc. (EMI Records)
Dr. John Plays Mac Rebbenack	Dr. John. (Rounder Records) Solo piano. (Clean Cuts Records)
Essential Blues Piano	Great blues piano compilation with Otis Spann, Lafayette Leake, Pinetop Perkins, Katie Webster, etc. (House of Blues)
Hoochie Coochie Man/ Got My Mojo Workin'	Jimmy Smith. (Verve Records)
Jump Back Honey	Hadda Brooks. The complete OKeh sessions (Columbia)
Live and Well Live at the Reggae	B.B. King. (MCA Records)
New Orleans Piano	Professor Longhair. (Atlantic)
Memphis Slim	Memphis Slim. (Chess MCA Records)
Patriarch of the Blues	Sunnyland Slim. (Opal Records)
Rekooperation	Al Kooper. (BMG Music)
Spiders on the Keys	James Booker (Rounder)
Texas Flood	Stevie Ray Vaughan. (Epic records). Classic example of modern blues guitar.
The Blues Never Die	Otis Spann. (Prestige Records)
The Chess 50th Anniversary Collection	Muddy Waters. (Chess/MCA Records)
The Complete Recordings	Robert Johnson. No keyboards here, but he may be the most important blues artist ever. (Columbia Records).
Vocal Accompaniment and Early Post-war Recordings: 1930-1954	Little Brother Montgomery. (Document Records)